## ALSO BY KAREN KINGSBURY

*The Family of Jesus*

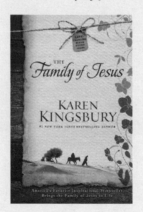

# The Friends of Jesus

## KAREN KINGSBURY

HOWARD BOOKS
An Imprint of Simon & Schuster, Inc.
New York   Nashville   London   Toronto   Sydney   New Delhi

Howard Books
An Imprint of Simon & Schuster, Inc.
1230 Avenue of the Americas
New York, NY 10020

Published in association with the literary agency of Alive Literary Agency, 7680 Goddard Street, Suite 200, Colorado Springs, Colorado, 80920, www.alivecommunications.com.

First Howard Books trade paperback edition July 2016

HOWARD and colophon are trademarks of Simon & Schuster, Inc.

For information about special discounts for bulk purchases, please contact Simon & Schuster Special Sales at 1-866-506-1949 or business@simonandschuster.com.

The Simon & Schuster Speakers Bureau can bring authors to your live event. For more information or to book an event, contact the Simon & Schuster Speakers Bureau at 1-866-248-3049 or visit our website at www.simonspeakers.com.

Interior design by Davina Mock-Maniscalco

Manufactured in the United States of America

10  9  8  7  6  5  4  3

Library of Congress Cataloging-in-Publication Data is available.

ISBN 978-1-4767-0739-6
ISBN 978-1-5011-4311-3 (pbk)
ISBN 978-1-4767-0747-1 (ebook)

*Dedicated to . . .*

Donald, who has always believed in the importance of Scripture. Thank you for introducing me to the Bible all those years ago. My entire life would be different without God's word . . . and without you. I love you always. How could a girl who once threw your Bible and broke the binding be writing stories about the friends of Jesus? Thanks for putting up with me all those years ago. God is faithful beyond words.

Kelsey, Kyle, Tyler, Sean, Josh, EJ, and Austin. May you always know the great love your father and I have for Jesus and His word, and may you be anchored and rooted in Scripture, passionate for our Lord always. I love you with all I am.

And most of all to God Almighty, who has—for now—blessed me with these.

# Contents

Introduction ix

1. Simon, the Leper
. . . And Jesus, the Compassionate Friend 1

2. Martha, the Broken-Hearted
. . . And Jesus, the Comforting Friend 41

3. Jairus, the Two-Faced Leader
. . . And Jesus, the Loyal Friend 75

4. Mary Magdalene, the Demon-Possessed
. . . And Jesus, the Friend Who Restores 103

5. Peter, the Betrayer
. . . And Jesus, the Friend Who Forgives 143

6. John, the Arrogant Disciple
. . . And Jesus, the Friend Who Transforms
Through Love 191

Acknowledgments 219

# Introduction

Before reading *The Friends of Jesus*, there are a few things you should know so that you might better understand the purpose of this book. I want you to know how you should step into these stories, how you should wrestle with them and analyze them and let them touch your heart.

First, I'm a storyteller. I write fiction. I see a single photo and a novel comes to life. A two-minute conversation can inspire a series. Second, I love the Bible. I base my life on the truths planted between the covers, and I would never do anything to violate Scripture.

That said, in *The Friends of Jesus* you will journey with me into the land of what might have been. The fact is, the people in the life of Jesus were real. They had real struggles and strengths, deeply emotional moments, and times when they rebelled.

I want you to better see the friends of Jesus, better know the reasons they were drawn to Him. And as you become more familiar with who these six friends of Jesus might've been and what might've motivated them, then I believe something wonderful will happen.

You'll want to spend more time in the Bible. You'll see

it as very real, and you'll see yourself between the lines. When Jesus extends His hand to Simon the Leper, you'll feel Him extending His hand to you.

Here's what you need to remember. I see these stories like beautiful tents dotting the landscape of a vast desert. The tent stakes are Scripture. They are unmovable, unshakable. Nothing written here will go against Scripture.

The rest, though, is like the canvas billowing in the wind between the tent stakes. That's where I step in. The stories you are about to read are fiction. I researched Scripture, culture, history, and the time period and wrote stories that are possible. I ran them by experts and they agreed. Yes, the way these friends of Jesus are depicted here is possible.

Of course, there were many friends of Jesus in the Bible. I simply chose these six because they are interesting to me. They represent diverse character traits and varying degrees of closeness to Jesus. They illustrate lessons about friendship that resonate in my heart. And there's something else about these six friends of Jesus.

I think you'll see yourself in one of them.

## CHAPTER 1

# Simon, the Leper

### . . . And Jesus, the Compassionate Friend

*If only he could get* away from the smell. The putrid, oppressive, nauseating smell. Simon sat on the edge of a craggy rock and looked out over the leper colony. How in the world had he wound up here? Banished from society, ostracized even by the people he loved? Dead to the world?

*Couldn't You send a breeze, God? So the smell wouldn't suffocate me?* He lifted his face and tried to peer through the menacing clouds. *Are You up there? Do You see me?*

*Never mind.* Simon closed his eyes. The other lepers kept to themselves. Here in the colony, everyone suffered in his own way. Missing family, aching for companionship. Too broken to notice the lepers on either side of him. And so Simon was alone. He who had been one of the most well-known men in Jerusalem had no one to love, no one to talk to, no one to care. His family had deserted him. He had no friends.

No one cared about Simon now. Not one.

Agony swept over him and he studied his hands. His fingers had turned to nubs—not that he could feel them. Leprosy took away the sense of pain everywhere but where it mattered most—in his heart. The pain of loneliness and desperation was more unbearable every day.

His eyes moved up his arms. Every inch of his body was open wounds or tumors. His feet no longer worked properly and his breathing was difficult. He prayed death wouldn't be far off. He must look like a monster, unrecognizable by human standards. He gritted his teeth. *It's more than I can take, Lord. Why have You done this to me?*

He opened his mouth to breathe. Sometimes if he drew air through his open lips he could avoid the stink—for a little while anyway. It was the one part of leprosy no one had told him about. The way his melting flesh would smell.

Thunder rumbled in the distance, an approaching storm almost upon them. Simon uttered a sad sigh. No, that was wrong. The storm had been crashing in on him since the day he first noticed the sores. He hadn't escaped the storm for a single minute. Simon hardly feared the lightning about to break through the sky overhead. If God wanted to strike him dead here on this rock, so be it. Anything to end his misery.

Then, like he'd done every hour of every day since he'd

been sent away, he allowed himself to go back in time, back to life the way it had been. Back when he was healthy and took the hours for granted. When he was surrounded by his wife, Anna, and their two young daughters. He closed his eyes and he could hear their voices, their laughter. The girls were eleven and twelve, adept at cooking and sewing and on the brink of becoming women. Back then they loved Simon more than life.

The ache in his heart was more crippling than his decaying flesh.

Anna hadn't wanted to leave. The girls wept and begged their mother for another option, a way for the family to stay together. But the disease wouldn't allow it. When Simon was escorted to the leper colony, his family—like families of other lepers—grieved his loss as if he had died.

He was dead to them, and they were encouraged to move on. Find a new life without him.

Simon wondered how they were doing now. Had they indeed moved on? Would Anna forget about him in time? He could see their faces again, feel his wife in his arms once more. *Anna, I still love you. I always will. Tell the girls I miss them.*

Simon still had no idea how he could've contracted leprosy. In his past life, no one had lived a better life than he had. He was a Pharisee, after all. The most important of the Jewish religious leaders. One of those entrusted with passing the law on to the next generation. And of course, a Pharisee could not teach the law unless he kept a strict adherence to it himself.

Simon had done everything right. He washed himself before every meal, sometimes more often. He kept the Sabbath holy, he fasted frequently, and he wore the best garments and tassels. He did everything in his power to uphold the law and he constantly pointed out those that failed to do so.

He could remember a time when three men were carrying spoons weighing more than a fig—a violation of the law. Simon had ordered them to leave the spoons on the side of the road. Another time he had publicly reprimanded a woman for working to find food for her children on the Sabbath. Any other day, but not the Sabbath.

Simon mulled over his behavior. Yes, he had been perfect. Quite. In all his days as a Pharisee he never ate with tax collectors or sinners. In fact, Simon wanted nothing more than to live a life that pleased God. The very word *Pharisee* had its root in purity, right?

And yet, one morning a year ago everything had changed. He would never forget those days. He could feel the solid comfortable ground of home beneath his feet, smell the bread cooking in the next room, hear the voices of Anna and the girls. And he could feel a slight burning on his arm. Just the slightest painful burning. Like something was biting or pinching him. Or like an ember from the fire had landed on him and taken root.

He could remember the sense of alarm as he looked at the underneath area of his forearm and first saw the open wound. Small and round, red and hot to the touch.

And then a second spot—up near his elbow, larger than the first.

Not for a moment did he think he had leprosy. Something must have bitten him during the night—a spider or a rare insect, maybe. Or perhaps he'd lingered too close to the fire and now he had the burn marks to prove it. Either way he wore his heavier cloak that day, the one with the tassels and longer arms that hung partway down his hand. He was a Pharisee. He couldn't have people wondering what was on his skin.

Especially since an outbreak of leprosy had recently hit Jerusalem.

Simon knew the signs, of course. He and his peers were part of the leadership team that cast lepers out of the Temple, out of the city. They were judge and jury, and for that reason Simon—more than other citizens—knew the symptoms. He knew exactly what to look for.

Of course he couldn't have leprosy.

But just in case, Simon prayed. *God, whatever this is, take it away. Leprosy is for the unclean, so I know I don't have that terrible disease. But whatever this is, please, take it away.* He said the prayer a few times that day, fully expecting that in the morning his arm would be well. Instead, three more sores had appeared near the existing ones. Open sores, oozing from the center. Not only that, but there were spots on his other arm. And two on his leg. All of them burned. Like someone was pressing the blade of a knife to his skin and scraping. Scraping and burrowing and ripping at him all day long.

Simon doubled his prayers, pleading with God to remove the spots. He didn't have leprosy. But still, if anyone saw the sores they might be confused and he could easily be mistaken for a leper. Which was impossible, because lepers were outcasts, people who had sinned against God and now were getting their just punishment. He was not such a sinner, and he was not a leper. Those thoughts had comforted Simon through the hours back then.

Early on he kept his distance from Anna. He went to bed after her and started his day earlier. He couldn't bear having her see the sores and wonder what was wrong. But over the next days and weeks Simon's skin condition grew worse. There were more spots, and then a white dusting that appeared over all his body. And finally one morning Simon woke to find his beard turning white.

The white that was a telltale sign of leprosy.

"Simon?" Anna had found him near their bed, examining his arms and legs. "What's happened to you?"

"It's nothing." He grabbed his cloak and threw it over himself. "Burns, maybe. Bites. We need to sweep for spiders."

"But your beard . . ." She took a step closer. "Simon, it's white as snow. Overnight. It looks like . . ." Her eyes were wide, her breathing faster than before. She had never looked more terrified.

"Anna . . . it's not like it looks." He reached for her, but maybe without thinking she took a step back.

His own wife. As if the very sight of him repulsed her.

Simon wanted to hide himself behind a wall or order

Anna from the room. He wanted the nightmare to end so he could wake up whole and well with Anna at his side and all of life perfectly planned and ahead of them.

But he could do none of that.

Simon slept on the floor that night, and after that there had been no way to hide the symptoms. The next day he had to report to duty in the Temple courts. As he walked through the groups of religious leaders he felt their stares, heard their whispered concern. Pharisees didn't get leprosy, unless . . .

Simon had almost been able to read their minds, the things they must've been thinking. What had Simon done? Why had he gone from being a perfectly upstanding Pharisee to this . . . this infected human being? Simon did his best to ignore the way they drew back from him. He walked straight to the rulers of the Temple.

"Can we talk?" He motioned to a back room. "Somewhere private. Please."

Jairus and the other rulers, the leaders of the Temple, seemed taken aback. They were Simon's closest friends, but now they looked him up and down and slowly they stepped back, keeping their distance. Clearly they noticed the sores on Simon's face, the white in his beard. With great hesitation they led Simon to a private place near the back of the Temple.

When they were alone, Jairus crossed his arms. "Simon. You are sick."

"Yes." Simon bowed slightly. "It's . . . an infection. Something must have bitten me or . . ." He hesitated.

What could he tell them? He knew the symptoms as well as they did. But even so he had never believed it could be leprosy. Not for him. "I'm sorry. Maybe a batch of weeds in the field has caused irritation. Or perhaps I stood too close to the fire. It could be that I—"

"Simon." Jairus held up his hand. "Remove your cloak."

Simon had feared they would say this. His beard gave it away. Until his beard turned white, he had been able to hide the patches of wounds cropping up on his arms and legs. But now . . .

He had shuddered at the thought of doing what Jairus asked. But he had no choice. Slowly, Simon removed his cloak, undressing himself to his undercloak. As he did, the leaders stepped back. One of them made an audible gasp. "Simon . . . you have leprosy."

"No!" Simon shook his head. "I've done nothing wrong. I've . . . I've kept all the commands of the laws." A desperate groan came from deep inside him. "I am a Pharisee. I could not possibly be unclean!"

And so the leaders of the Temple had quickly conferred. They agreed they'd never before seen a religious leader with leprosy. "Perhaps you are dealing with an allergy." One of the leaders nodded. "We would like to think so, anyway."

Jairus and the others came up with a plan, something they often did for members of the Temple who were brought to them with symptoms of leprosy. They sent Simon home for two weeks. "Your family should stay with relatives. You must be alone, and do not leave your house for any reason." One of the leaders seemed more compassionate. "Surely your wounds will heal in that time. Your family can join you again and you can return to your duties at the Temple."

Simon made arrangements for his wife and girls to stay with her brother a half-day's walk away. Anna had talked to him from a distance before she left. "You will heal, Simon. I will pray to God. It'll be okay." She looked scared and heartbroken. As if she didn't for a moment believe her own words.

The girls had cried, wanting to go to him and hug him. But Anna held them back. "Later, girls. After your father is well."

And with that, they were gone.

Simon had known with everything in him that two weeks was all he needed. His skin would heal and the horrific, impossible thought of leprosy would disappear with the wounds.

He was convinced. But he was wrong.

*The storm moved closer,* dark, menacing clouds headed Simon's way. He breathed through his mouth, sick to his stomach from his stench. The memory of those early days when everything went bad played in his mind every day. Sometimes every hour. Ahead a little ways, lightning split the sky and hit the ground. Simon didn't move. If the lightning didn't kill him, at least the storm would bring relief, fresh air to soothe his lungs from breathing only the putrid smell of his rotting flesh.

He closed his eyes and let the past come over him again.

Those two weeks had been the most frightening in all his life. Every day he prayed and every morning he woke expecting to be healed. But the sores didn't go away. They grew larger and deeper. More of them appeared every sunrise. One week into his time of quarantine, Simon climbed out of bed, took two steps, and fell, sprawled across the dirt floor. He couldn't feel his feet, and as he looked down he saw the sickening reality. His toes were turning white. They were dying, right before his eyes.

Which could only mean one thing.

In the days that followed he prayed constantly. Every hour. What had he done wrong? Why would God inflict him with something so horrific? He repented for things he couldn't remember doing and begged God to forgive him for thoughts he didn't know he had considered. Surely he must've disobeyed or disappointed God. Whatever he'd done, he was sorry. He would repent the rest of his life if God would only heal him.

But every day his condition grew worse.

His sores itched and burned. He could no longer feel his fingers and toes. And something else. Tumors had started appearing on his arms and legs and even on his face and torso. Lumps the size of large olives pressed up against his broken, oozing skin. The tumors made his whole body throb. As if even his bones were decaying.

Simon noticed something else that week. His bed had begun to stink. Each morning it was covered with sections of his white, shedding skin. The floor of the house bore telltale signs of the same. He was becoming a leper, a monster. An outcast. And there was nothing he could do about it. No way to stop the destruction.

After his two weeks alone, the morning came to report to the leaders of the Temple. Simon had never felt more desperate. He woke early and dropped to his painful knees. Everything hurt—his joints and limbs and every inch of his skin.

"Lord, I am here! Have You abandoned me?" His prayer echoed through his empty house. "I have kept Your law, I have followed Your ways. Why have You not healed me?"

And then—for the first time since he started praying about his condition, he felt the gentlest whisper. A whisper that surrounded him.

*My son, this has been done to show My glory to the people of Jerusalem.*

Simon could remember feeling breathless. Was that really God speaking to him? God was at the center of the law, the reason Simon lived a perfect life as a Pharisee. But God speaking to him? In the quiet of his room? He had never experienced such a thing. He hunkered down against his bed, small in the presence of the voice of God.

What had the voice said? God was doing this to show His glory? How could that be? No one in the vicinity of Jerusalem kept the law the way Simon did. Others could try, but Simon had been perfect. He prided himself on the fact. He deserved his place as a Pharisee. So how could God be glorified by giving him this wicked disease?

For the next hour he cried out to God, begging the Lord to remember his perfect service, his perfect commitment to the law. His perfect way of serving in the Temple. Begging Him to recall the fact that he was a Pharisee. But God didn't speak to him again that morning. When it came time to report before the religious leaders, Simon was no better off. His healing had not come. As if God had forgotten all the good and right things Simon had ever done.

He covered up as well as he could that morning and headed to the Temple. Walking was difficult, but he managed it. He could feel the way the people of the city stared at him as he passed by. It didn't matter how much his cloak covered. His face had spots now, and his beard was whiter than before.

When he stepped into the Temple, people cleared a wide path for him. This time he heard the word in their whispers. *Leper. Simon is a leper.* No one said a thing to him as he slowly, carefully moved to the back of the Temple. He didn't think of the pain in his feet. His heart pounded in his throat as he made his way. How could this be happening? It seemed to take forever to reach the private meeting place.

Jairus and the other leaders were waiting.

As Simon approached them he remembered dozens of times with these very men. Times of laughter and fellowship. Meals and conversations about the law. Pleasant hours of study and intense debate. These men were his friends. But that morning they kept their distance. As Simon approached, Jairus held up his hand. "That's close enough."

Simon stopped and waited. The floor beneath him felt liquid, and his balance was unsteady. Each of them began to assess Simon's condition. Their words of condemnation ran together but there were no surprises. They asked him once more to remove his cloak, and then—after their shocked gasps—they made the pronouncement.

"Whatever you have done, Simon, it must be very grievous indeed. You have leprosy. You show all the symptoms."

"That's impossible!" Simon lifted his hands in emphasis, but he already knew. He lowered his hurting arms and stared at his friends. His life was in their hands. "I have done nothing to make myself unclean."

Jairus shook his head. "Your words are meaningless. Your skin gives you away, Simon." He paused, the weight of what he was about to say heavy in the small room. "You know what must happen next. Your wife and daughters will return to your home for a final goodbye. You will gather your necessities and move to the leper colony outside the city. Isaac and Joseph will escort you to the entrance." He sighed. "Unless by some miracle you are healed, you are not to return, Simon. I'm sorry."

"This cannot be!" *Isaac and Joseph?* They were Pharisees, two of Simon's closest friends. "Sir, I haven't done—"

"Stop!" Jairus looked stern, almost angry. "No more excuses, Simon. Remember what the law requires regarding leprosy." He paused, clearly disgusted by Simon's condition. "Wherever you go, you will cover your mouth and call out 'Unclean.' Every time you pass someone, or if someone passes by you. Don't forget."

Every word hit Simon like a bullet.

Anna and the girls met him back home while Isaac and Joseph waited outside. The girls tried to run to him, but Anna wouldn't let them. "Wait by the door, girls." They started crying, but they did as their mother asked. Anna turned to Simon and came closer. She stopped when she was still quite a distance away. Tears filled her eyes. "I cannot believe this is happening."

"Me, either." His body felt like it was on fire. But the pain was nothing to the searing loss in his heart. "I'll get better, Anna. I will."

Her tears came harder. "Jairus gave the orders. We're to view you as dead, Simon."

*Dead?* Nausea washed over Simon. That meant Anna would be treated as a widow. She would be encouraged to forget him. As if he'd never been born. He couldn't bear the thought. Desperate, he held out his oozing hands to her. "Anna . . . I love you. I'll get better, I will."

She was weeping now, and she hung her head. There was nothing more to say. After a few gut-wrenching seconds, she called the girls to her side. "Tell your father goodbye."

"No!" Miriam, their oldest shook her head. "We can't leave him! He needs our help!"

From outside the house, Isaac shouted, "It's time!"

Anna put her arms around the girls. She took a step backward. "Goodbye, Simon."

The girls cried out, screaming for some other way, destroyed at the idea that this was goodbye. The last time they might ever see their father. Forever. Simon fell to his knees as Anna pulled them away. "I love you!" he shouted. "I will always love you!"

When they were gone, Simon buried his face in the dirt. His shoulders shook from the sobs exploding within him. "God, why? Why me?" He yelled the word through his tears, gasping for air.

"Simon, now!" It was Joseph this time. His old friend had come in the house and now he stood near the doorway, his face a mask of disgust. "Let's go."

Simon gritted his teeth. Dirt from the floor mixed with his sticky saliva and made it hard for him to swallow. He would not let this be a final goodbye. Healing would come. God could do that, right? And when He did, Simon would return and claim again all that he'd lost.

Isaac and Joseph were yelling at him again, telling him to hurry. Simon gathered a bag of clothes and personal items and left his home. He didn't look back. He couldn't. The pain was too great. Every step felt like he was stepping through fire and his heart was somewhere behind him. Lying on the floor at the spot where he'd said goodbye to his wife and daughters.

As he moved through Jerusalem, two women approached and Simon's escorts raised their brows in his direction.

"Unclean," Simon muttered.

"Louder," Isaac sneered at him. "Much louder."

"Unclean! I'm unclean!" Simon shouted the words, and for the first time the reality sank in. He was unclean. It was true. After that, every time he passed someone he shouted the warning, "Unclean!" He yelled as loud as he could. "Unclean . . . unclean!"

Simon wondered if he might collapse before he reached the leper colony that day. He even wondered if maybe God would heal him before he reached the forsaken place. Instead his feet were bleeding, unable to handle the long walk to the edge of the city. None of it was fair. He hadn't done anything to deserve leprosy.

He held on to that one thought as Isaac and Joseph left him, and as Simon took his first steps through the entrance of the leper colony. One thought consumed him as his friends walked away.

This was the first miserable day of the rest of his life.

As the past played out, Simon searched desperately for the error in his ways. Where had he so completely failed? Why had God done this to him?

No matter how hard he examined the details leading up to his sickness, however often he repented for things he hadn't done and things he hadn't thought, the truth was he'd done nothing wrong. He'd committed no sin or violation of the law. He had been perfect. Of course he had been. He was a Pharisee. Nothing less than perfection was expected from a man in his position.

Thunder shook the ground beneath him. The storm

was nearly overhead, and rain began falling. Hard rain. The kind that could flood ravines and gullies. Simon didn't care. He stayed on the rock. If the rain fell hard enough he might actually feel it through his dead skin. He sucked in a full breath and felt a satisfaction that had eluded him for weeks.

Wind from the storm had almost taken away his terrible stink. Almost. His lungs filled with the rich aroma of the storm. Rain and dirt and flowers from the distant field all mixed together and bathed his senses with a delight he rarely experienced. *Let the storm come, God. Let it take me.*

Lightning struck closer still and again Simon wished it would hit him. He might go to hell for whatever he had done, whatever had caused this horrific abomination. But at least he could escape his rotting body.

Certainly hell would be better than this.

*The storm passed quickly* and the lightning did not kill him. In its wake, the air was still and warm. The smell worse than ever. Simon sat on the rocky ledge, not moving, not sure what to do. *You must be very angry at me, God. You have taken my livelihood, my place of honor, my family and my friends. My wife is probably a different person by now. My girls have forgotten me. It's been nearly a year. And yet here You leave me in this leper colony to watch my body decay piece by piece? I just want to know why.*

His rants toward God were nearly constant now. God

could heal him—Simon believed that. Yet God had left him here, as if He had forgotten entirely about Simon and his awful disease. Simon was about to let his mind go back again to the past, back to the days before the sores appeared. About to search, over and over again, for his sin and the reason he'd been banished, when he heard a commotion in the distance.

A group of travelers must have been making its way along the edge of the colony. Clearly they were unaware this was a leper colony. Otherwise they wouldn't pass so close. Simon watched as the lepers noticed the traveling group. A stir passed through the sickly, disfigured men and a series of cries rose from amidst the group. "Unclean! Unclean! Unclean!"

The sound grew louder, warning the passersby. Normally, if foreigners wandered too close to the leper colony, as soon as they heard the cries from the unclean people, they would run for their lives. As far away as they could get. It still wasn't clear how leprosy passed from one person to another. Most people believed it was simply a punishment from God, a way of giving outward expression to the inward sin that certainly must have taken root. Still, no one wanted to take chances. And so healthy people kept their distance.

Only this time the group did not run. Simon sat a little straighter on the rock and peered at those approaching the colony. Couldn't they hear the warning cries? What were they doing? This was the strangest thing he'd seen since he'd been here. The group was actually coming closer. One of them—a man tall and strong—seemed to be their leader. He had a dozen men around him.

Whatever was happening, Simon needed to be nearer to the scene. He slowly tried to climb down off the rock. His toes were gone now, but he had learned to navigate his way without them. Unsteady. Uncertain. Simon picked up speed, but he still wasn't fast. After just ten steps, he tripped on a rock and fell hard to the ground. The sores on his arm began to bleed. His bones showed through some of his wounds, but Simon didn't care. He had to get to the edge of the colony.

To the place where the travelers were coming closer.

Finally he scrambled to a spot partially hidden behind a bush. A murmur came from the crowd of lepers. *Jesus.* The man leading the group of travelers was Jesus? Disdain and curiosity mixed together in Simon's soul. Jesus of Nazareth? The one they called Teacher? Simon squinted in His direction. Jesus stopped and looked intently at the colony of lepers, at the men shouting, "Unclean!" The Teacher seemed overcome by sorrow. He hung His head, and when He looked at the lepers, tears filled His eyes. As if the sight of the diseased men actually broke His heart.

Simon blinked, confused. He had never seen Jesus this close up, but certainly he knew of Him. All the religious leaders knew of Him. Jesus the miracle worker. Jesus the healer. Jesus who claimed to be God Almighty.

The one who actually believed He was the Messiah.

Before his sickness, Simon had attended the meetings, the ones where the religious leaders discussed their

frustration and dislike of Jesus. The Pharisees and Sadducees disagreed about many things. But they agreed every
time there was another report about the Teacher and His
followers. The consensus was clear: Jesus was not the
Messiah. When the Messiah came, He would come in
glory. With an entourage of royalty. He would be a mighty
force against the oppressive Roman government, and He
would set His people free.

Once and for all.

This Jesus had it all backward. His followers included
peasants and sinners. Tax collectors and dirty fishermen.
He wore the ragged clothes of a carpenter. Clearly Jesus
was not God in the flesh. When the religious leaders
talked about plans to kill Jesus, Simon heartily agreed.
How dare this son of a carpenter claim to be God? How
dare He confuse the people in Jerusalem and the surrounding areas?

But here, now, Simon was mesmerized by Jesus.
Drawn to Him, to the kindness in His eyes. Jesus waited
until the crowd of lepers quieted. One of the sick men
raised a fist in Jesus's direction. "Don't you know who we
are, Jesus of Nazareth? Be gone from here!"

Jesus came a step closer. His followers stayed at a distance, concern written in the lines on their faces.

"Unclean!" one of the lepers yelled. "Unclean!"

Then Jesus did the strangest thing. When He should've
kept walking, He held out His hands. Held them out to the
entire colony of lepers. Suddenly two lepers approached
Him, moving closer to Jesus. Simon could barely draw a

breath as he watched. The men were missing hands and feet. They walked only with the help of large sticks. Their faces were grotesquely disfigured, and flakes of skin fell from them as they approached Him.

His disciples stepped further back.

But Jesus didn't flinch. He kept His arms spread out toward the men. Then He motioned to the other lepers, as if to invite them, also.

Another terribly disfigured man stepped up and then four joined him and three more. Ten in all. They looked at each other and with a boldness that betrayed logic they came to Jesus.

The Teacher had time to turn and walk away, time to order the lepers to halt and not come a step closer. But instead Jesus looked at them with compassion. With a kindness lepers had long since forgotten.

"Come." Jesus looked at each of the men. "Come to Me all you who are weary and burdened."

*Weary and burdened?* Simon felt an ache in his heart. No one had cared for the lepers since they'd been banished to this forsaken colony. But here, Jesus defined their condition in those two words. Weary and burdened.

Weary with sickness, weary with the smell of rotting flesh. Burdened with the judgment of sinfulness and the label: *Unclean. Unclean. Unclean.* Weary from being alone. Burdened with the absence of friends, the loss of family.

Surprise showed on the rotting faces of the ten lepers. Jesus had called them close and so these ten seemed determined to come. They hobbled nearer and, as they reached arm's distance from Jesus, one at a time they bowed their heads, unsteady on what was left of their feet. Whatever these men had thought about Jesus before, one thing was clear now.

They believed He was the Healer. They seemed desperate to believe.

"Jesus! Jesus!" they began to cry out. "Master, have pity on us."

Simon's shock was so great he could barely focus. These men not only believed Jesus was the Healer—they had called Him the Master. Could these ten lepers believe that Jesus was God Almighty? The expected Messiah? Emmanuel?

For more than a year before his sickness, Simon had been trained to believe Jesus was a heretic. A false prophet. Simon stared at the Teacher, at the gentleness that exuded from Him. Suddenly a thought occurred to Simon. What if he had been wrong about Jesus? What if all the religious leaders had been wrong?

For several minutes the lepers called out words of worship—hosanna in the highest, hallelujah to the Messiah. Together they begged Jesus to have mercy on them. Finally Jesus held up His hand and the lepers fell silent. "Go and show yourselves to the priests."

Simon thought he was hidden by the bush. But as Jesus said the word "priests," He turned. And He looked straight into the eyes of Simon. He needed no words. It was as if He were saying, "I see you, Simon. I know that you were once a priest."

A gasp came from Simon, and he thought about running. But he couldn't move. Couldn't do anything but remain there under the intense and compassionate gaze of Jesus.

Then the Teacher turned to the lepers once more and did something that brought an audible cry of alarm from the crowd. He started with the first disfigured man and without any sense of disgust or fear, Jesus put His hand on the man's shoulder.

He touched the leprous, putrid skin of the leper.

Something no one would dare do, Jesus did. He walked slowly down the line of ten diseased men and one at a time, He touched them. Placed His clean hand on the unclean shoulder of each of them. And as He did, He spoke the words once more. "Go now. Do as I said. Show yourselves to the priests."

A sad, compassionate smile lifted the corners of Jesus's lips as He stepped back. The way He looked at the lepers was almost as a father might look at his sick children. Care and concern. Longing for healing. Jesus gave a final nod and then returned to His followers.

The twelve wore mixed expressions. Some of His disciples looked proud of their Master. Others looked horrified by what He had done. The way He had touched the unclean men. Still, each found his place alongside Jesus as the group departed in the direction of Jerusalem.

Something in Simon screamed out. Should he hurry after Jesus? Maybe his only chance at healing was walking away. But he couldn't make himself move. The lepers were not healed, after all. They still stood there, broken and disfigured. Their flesh still literally falling off their bones.

Then one of them looked at the other nine. "He told us to go." He pointed to Jerusalem. "I'm going."

As he moved forward, the others looked around and then one at a time they hobbled after the first man. As they left, the name of Jesus was on their lips and the sound lifted like a powerful breeze through the leper colony. "Jesus said so . . . Jesus is the Healer . . . I'm going where Jesus said to go . . ."

The ten were not a handful of steps into their journey to see the priests of Jerusalem when they began to change. Right before the eyes of everyone in the colony, the skin of the ten began to heal. Their beards became dark again and their limbs reappeared. New fingers where nubs had been. Fresh feet and ankles in place of stumps. New flesh, unblemished.

In a handful of seconds all ten lepers were healed.

A few seconds passed before even the lepers realized what had happened. Then all at once they began leaping and jumping and shouting praises to God. Jesus had healed them! He had ordered them to go to the priests because He knew they would be healed along the way. They were made whole the moment they obeyed Him.

Simon slowly sank to the ground. All around the colony the remaining lepers called out, yelling praises to God on behalf of the ten men. All Simon could think was the obvious. Since the lepers were completely healed—since all ten were well again—Jesus must be the Healer.

And if He was the Healer then it was possible He was who He said He was. And that could only mean . . .

The thought paralyzed Simon.

He brought his nubby fingers to his face and felt tears in his eyes. If Jesus was the Healer, then He was also the Messiah. False prophets didn't touch lepers and heal them. The religious leaders were wrong about Jesus. Forget the anticipated entourage of royalty. Forget the hoped-for kingly attire and the expected powerful push against the Roman government. Never mind how it appeared.

Jesus was the Messiah.

Suddenly Simon was absolutely convinced. The evidence of his eyes was too great to ignore. But at the same time a grievous thought occurred to him. He had missed his chance! Jesus had stood before the colony of lepers and only ten men had come forward. Only ten with the faith to believe that maybe—just maybe—Jesus could heal them.

And Simon was not one of them. He had stood twenty feet from the Messiah and hid in the bushes. Even when Jesus looked him straight in the eyes Simon had done nothing but remain hidden. The weight of his shame hit him like boulders raining down on his warped back.

If he ever had another chance, if Jesus ever happened by the leper colony again, he would run to Him with all his strength. Simon looked at the distant storm clouds retreating along the horizon. *Please, God . . . give me another chance. I'm sorry. I believe. I do believe.*

No matter what happened next, Simon knew this much.

He would never doubt Jesus again.

*The days that followed* were slow and full of questions. Not only for Simon but for the other men in the colony. They had all seen the miraculous healing of the ten, and now each had his own theory about how it could've happened. Some believed it was a trick, part of a scheme by Jesus and His followers. Others believed as Simon did, that Jesus was the Messiah.

For the most part Simon kept to himself. His smell was horrific, so he spent most of his hours on the ledge of the rock, a few feet above the colony. The only place where he could think and remember and ponder how he had gotten here. The only place where he could pray to God that Jesus of Nazareth might pass their way once more.

Just once.

Two weeks after the healing of the ten, Simon noticed something. The fingers on his left hand were entirely gone. They must've fallen off while he slept. The pain of leprosy no longer plagued him. He could fall into a fire and he wouldn't notice it. Proof that he didn't have long. Eventually the leprosy would eat him from the outside in. It would destroy his organs, eat away at his heart and lungs and brain. One morning he would simply not wake up.

And that would be that.

Unless . . .

He pictured Jesus again, the kindness He exuded, the calm way He had about Him. Then he remembered the Master's twelve followers. There seemed nothing special about the men. They were not powerful or politicians. None of them were religious leaders. Simon doubted that combined they had half the knowledge he did about the laws and ordinances of the Jewish faith.

Yet they were given the greatest privilege of all.

The privilege of being friends of Jesus.

What must it have been like to be a friend of Jesus? To walk with Him and talk to Him. To stand ringside to every miracle Jesus had performed for the desperate people in His path? How wonderful to eat with Him and hear Jesus declare God's word. Because He was God. God. In the flesh.

The thought was more than Simon could imagine. If Jesus ever passed by, if Simon was somehow blessed enough to be healed by the Master, then he had one wish. One dream.

That Jesus might come to His house for a meal. That Jesus would be his friend. More than the healed flesh on his bones, more than his returned place in society, Simon longed for the friendship of Jesus. The religious leaders had never been his real friends. They were only friends in good times. When a person was perfect.

Jesus was the only One who did not judge and fear the lepers. The One who stepped forward and touched the unclean when everyone else hurried in the other direction. Simon wanted a friend like that. He wanted to *be* a friend like that.

And so he waited, sitting on his rock. From that vantage point the smell was slightly less severe. But more important he could see the road that passed by the colony. If Jesus ever walked by again, Simon would be one of the first to see Him.

The sun beat down on his shoulders. There was no relief from the heat, no way to find respite of any kind. But still Simon sat. And rather than allow himself to remember the beginning again, Simon prayed. *God, if You would please bring Jesus by once more. I am sorry for not rushing forward when I had the chance. Jesus is the friend to the friendless, the One who looks past my disease. I know that now . . .*

As he prayed, Simon remembered the quiet whisper of God back when he first noticed lesions on his arms.

*My son, this has been done to show My glory to the people of Jerusalem.*

A breath of hope worked through his lungs. Maybe Jesus would return. Maybe not. But God had spoken to him back then. No matter what happened next.

He was reminding himself of that very thing when he heard the sound of travelers. His heart skipped a beat and he struggled to make his legs work. He had to see who was coming, who was headed this way from Jerusalem. Other lepers must've seen the caravan, too, because once more they cried out as they were required.

"Unclean! Unclean! Unclean!"

Simon found a way to stand. Was it Jesus? Could it be the Master?

Suddenly the travelers came into view. He couldn't be sure but it looked like maybe . . . just maybe . . .

He scrambled down the rock, falling to the ground. *Work, legs . . . you have to work. Please, God, if it's Jesus, let me go to Him.* Somehow he managed to get what remained of his feet beneath him. Gradually his hobbling steps became something that resembled a sprint. "Jesus!" he cried out even before he knew for sure.

And as he rounded the corner finally he could see clearly.

At the front of the group was Jesus. Master. Messiah. The Healer. The echoes of "Unclean!" stopped and the crowd stilled. Many were busy inside the colony, making food and going about their business. But those who came to the edge of the colony seemed too shocked to move.

All but Simon. He held out one deformed hand. "Jesus, wait! I believe! I do believe!"

Jesus stopped, and again His followers kept their distance. This time there was no hiding for Simon. He wanted Jesus to see him, all of him. His broken, lonely heart and his diseased body. He came up to Jesus and fell at His feet. "I need You, Lord! Have mercy on me. You are Master and Savior. Please heal me. I am desperate."

Simon closed his eyes and held out his hand. Maybe this was only a dream. How could Jesus be standing inches from him? He trembled, unable to draw a breath, and then when he thought he must've been imagining the moment, he felt it.

The touch of the Master's hand.

Jesus had taken hold of Simon's nubby wrist, as if Simon weren't missing fingers. As if his skin weren't falling off his bones. "Simon, My son. Open your eyes."

Simon did as he was told and what he saw was the most beautiful sight in all his life. Jesus was still holding his hand. "Simon, your faith has healed you. Go show yourself to the priests."

"Yes, Lord. I will. Yes." Simon stayed on his knees. He was in the presence of God. He could feel it to the depths of his soul.

Not one other leper came to Jesus. Simon looked back at the men. No one else came. Like they didn't believe or they didn't understand. Surely they knew Jesus was the Healer, the Messiah. But whatever the reason they kept their distance. Jesus hesitated, His eyes deep with sorrow. Then He turned and went on His way. At the same time, Simon began to feel something happening inside him. The feeling was wonderful and intense all at once and then, in a matter of seconds, he watched his hands grow back. Fingers reappeared as if they'd never been diseased. His arms and legs became smooth and healthy and strong, and the tumors all over his body disappeared.

Two of the lepers came close and one of them shouted, "It happened again! Jesus did this!"

Of course Jesus did this! Simon wanted to yell at his peers. How had they not believed, even after Jesus had healed the ten? Either way it didn't matter. He was no longer part of the leper colony.

He was healed.

By the touch of the Master's hand, he had been healed.

Simon left his things and rushed to the city gates. Clean again, he had no trouble passing through. Relief washed over him with every breath. His friends would welcome him back. He would be respected among his peers, invited to their dinners. He would find Anna and the girls and pray it wasn't too late to bring them home. He was healed! Simon ran to the Temple and rushed inside. The religious leaders were meeting, and all at once they looked up as he entered the building.

"Simon . . ." Jairus stood, his mouth open. "What . . . what happened?"

"It was Jesus!" Simon searched the faces of his former peers. "Jesus came by the leper colony and . . . He healed me!"

His pronouncement was met by silence. The Sadducees and Pharisees whispered among themselves, their faces dark with distrust. Suddenly Simon remembered. "The ten lepers! They came a few weeks ago. Surely you saw them. They were all healed by Jesus, and now I've been healed, too."

Jairus approached him. "Take off your cloak."

Simon was happy to comply. He ripped off his outer garment. "See?" He held out his arms to Jairus and then to his old friends. Isaac and Joseph stood just a few feet away. A relieved laugh came from Simon. "I've never been better. Jesus did this!"

No one said a word. Not Isaac. Not Joseph. No one.

Jairus nodded slowly. He was a man of great pride and confidence. He had a way of making the other religious leaders wish for his knowledge. He sneered. "And now, Simon . . . now do you believe Jesus is the Messiah?"

Another happy sound, part laugh, part cry, came from Simon. "Of course! He is Emmanuel. God with us." Again he held out his arms. "Isn't this proof?"

Jairus cleared his throat. "Simon, you are not welcome here. I'm sorry."

It took Simon a moment to realize what was happening. "Are you serious?"

"Yes." Jairus's face had no expression at all. "You need to go."

"Jairus!" Simon shook his head. "I'm healed! You . . ." He looked around the room. "You are my friends."

"No." Jairus shook his head. "We do not associate with lepers—healed or not!"

Simon's heart raced, his breathing came fast. "You still don't believe Jesus is who He says He is?"

"Absolutely not." Isaac stepped forward. "He is an impostor. We are making plans to eliminate Him."

"No!" Simon looked around the Temple at the Sadducees and Pharisees. "You can't do that. Jesus is kind and full of compassion. He is healing people every day, setting them free from demons. Everything the people say about Him, it's true! How could you want Him gone from here?"

"Simon." Jairus motioned for Simon to follow him. "You are aware of the town Bethany?"

"Bethany? Of course, but—"

"The sick live in Bethany," Jairus interrupted. "And that is where you must go now. You will find shelter there." He walked Simon to the door of the Temple. "Don't come back. And don't try to stop us. Whatever happens in the days and weeks ahead, remember this . . . we are acting in the best interest of Jerusalem."

"You can't harm Jesus. He's the Messiah and—"

"Don't speak." Jairus raised his voice. "We will do as we see fit." The man's expression held no room for negotiation. "Besides, Jesus is spending much time in Bethany. Maybe you will see Him there. And if you do"—a dark shadow fell over the man's eyes—"do not warn Him of our plans."

Simon tried to talk again, but he couldn't speak a word. He was too shocked to find his voice.

"Be gone, Simon." Jairus hesitated. "And don't look for Anna. She is remarried. You are to have no contact with her or your daughters. You are dead to them." Jairus pushed him from the Temple. "And to us."

Simon's legs and arms worked perfectly fine. Better than ever. But even so, Simon struggled to take a step. What had just happened? His wife and daughters were part of another family now? He hadn't been gone a full year. Simon's mind raced and he grabbed on to the nearest tree so he wouldn't collapse. He couldn't believe it. His peers, his friends, his former family—none of them had any intention of welcoming him back whether he was healed or not. All because Jesus had healed him.

And now they were making plans to harm Jesus?

What had Jairus said? Jesus was spending time in Bethany. Simon stood straighter and his steps became more determined. Fine. He would go to Bethany and find shelter. Then he would do what he longed to do.

He would find Jesus and thank Him.


*Bethany turned out to* be a place of respite for Simon. He became friends with a dear family—two sisters and their younger brother—Mary, Martha, and Lazarus. The three lived close by and they often met with Simon, sharing stories of their time with Jesus.

He was the Messiah. They were as convinced as Simon.

"But He is also our friend." Mary's eyes lit up. "There is no greater friend than Jesus."

Simon's life was so different now. Better. Gone were his priestly obligations. He now read and understood the Scriptures differently. They told about Jesus's coming. It had been right there, all along. But for the first time, Simon recognized Jesus. Also, Simon had found work, helping a farmer at the edge of Bethany. Every chance he had, he made his new home more welcoming. He had a table and chairs, places to recline and visit. If Jesus ever came through Bethany again, Simon planned to ask Him to dinner. He would return the favor of friendship.

It was the least he could do to thank Jesus for healing him that day.

One afternoon there was a knock at Simon's door. Could it be Jesus, come to share dinner with him? Simon hoped so, but as he answered the call instead there stood Jonah, one of the ten lepers who had been healed by Jesus that day at the edge of the leper colony. Jonah looked whole and well, same as Simon. He nodded. "May I come in?"

"Of course." Simon stepped aside and welcomed the man into his home. "You live in Bethany?"

"I do. I want to help the sick. I want to be like Jesus."

Simon understood. He felt the same way. "You . . . you've talked to Him? Since your healing?"

"I have." Jonah sat across from Simon at the table. "You won't believe what happened."

Then Jonah told a story Simon would remember forever. An awful story that shocked him and grieved him at the same time.

"After the ten of us were healed, we did as Jesus asked. We went to the priests and showed ourselves to be clean. We were declared whole again, healed. But when we told the priests that Jesus had healed us, they banned us from the Temple." Jonah paused. "For a few minutes, I wondered if the leaders might kill us."

Simon pictured Jairus, his former friends and peers. "It was the same for me."

Jonah seemed lost in thought, back again in that moment outside the Temple gates. "The ten of us stood there, shaking. We had no idea our healing would be a problem." He paused. "Some people ran by talking about Jesus. He was preaching a few blocks away." Jonah paused. "I was the first one to speak. I told the others we had to go find Jesus. Forget what the priests said. The ten of us had to thank Him!"

It was a beautiful picture. The ten outcast healed lepers making a plan to find Jesus and thank Him. Simon was gripped by the story. "So the group of you went?"

"No." Jonah's expression grew full of sorrow. "The other nine shook their heads. They were afraid of the priests. Terrified. They wanted nothing to do with Jesus!" Jonah stared out the window of Simon's house. "Jesus treated us like a friend. He touched us when no one else would come near us. Not even our families. But that day outside the Temple, the other nine were too afraid to tell Jesus thank you."

"That's awful." Simon was shocked. How could a person receive that sort of gift—a second chance at life—and let fear cripple him?

Jonah shook his head. "I haven't seen them since."

"What a loss for them." Simon leaned back in his chair. "So you moved here?"

"I wanted to be near Jesus. He loves the people of Bethany. He has friends here."

"Yes. They're my friends, too. Mary and Martha and Lazarus." Simon smiled. "All of us look for Jesus every day."

"He will be here soon. I've heard from many in town."

"I need to get word to Him." Joy came over Simon. No matter how many people were afraid to be associated with

Jesus, Simon wanted to be His friend. He would be here, door open, whenever Jesus passed by. Before Jonah left, Simon pleaded with him. "If you see Jesus, please . . . ask Him to come to my house. I want to give Him a meal and thank Him. I want to be the sort of friend to Him that He was to me."

Jonah smiled. "I'll tell Him."

A wonderful few weeks passed and though Simon grew closer to Mary and Martha and Lazarus, though he was able to help the sick and offer food to the poorest ones in Bethany, Jesus still did not pass through.

Worse, word from Jerusalem was that the Sadducees and Pharisees wanted to destroy Jesus. Now. Simon shuddered when he remembered the words of the eldest leader. They wanted to eliminate Jesus. They would do their best to see that it happened. Simon had no doubt.

As Passover drew near, the villagers of Bethany heard news that Jesus was returning to their community. Simon went to the house of Mary and Martha and Lazarus and left word. "If you see Jesus, tell Him to come by my house. Please."

Two more days slipped by and then one morning there was a knock at the door. Simon's heart raced as he opened it and there . . . there stood Jesus.

"Simon."

"My Lord." Simon fell to his knees. "Thank You. You healed me. I will forever be thankful."

Jesus reached out His hand and helped Simon to his feet. "May I come in?"

There was a crowd with Jesus, but Simon didn't care. This was Jesus his friend, his Master. His Savior and Healer. "Yes, my Lord. Please. All of you may come in. I'll prepare dinner now."

"Not now. Later. We will share a meal soon." Jesus smiled. "I still have work to do."

And so Jesus and His followers entered Simon's house and for a short while they visited. Jesus his Master. Jesus his friend. Before he left, Jesus hugged Simon.

"I want a new way from you, Simon. A way of grace and mercy. Love and truth. Truth lived out. I don't expect you to be perfect. Do you understand?"

"I think so, Lord." Simon hung on every word.

"I am the way, the truth and the life. No man comes to the Father except through Me."

No words had ever felt more true to Simon. "Yes, Lord. Thank You. For healing me. For being my friend."

Jesus smiled, and then He and His followers went on their way.

Simon could barely contain his joy. Jesus would come to eat with him one day soon. The way friends did. And as Simon went to sleep that night, he thought about his life, his past before being sick, and his happiness and gratitude since Jesus healed him.

Back before his illness, Simon had to be perfect. His friends at the Temple, the religious leaders, only enjoyed his company because he was a Pharisee. Because his performance was up to their standards. Because he followed the letter of the law.

Jesus asked about none of that.

As the Messiah, Jesus saw Simon as he was—a leper, bankrupt and in desperate need of healing. In need of the touch of someone who cared. Jesus was the sort of friend Simon had never known before. He didn't expect perfection from Simon. He only wanted Simon to believe. Jesus was the way, the truth and the life. He only wanted to show Simon this new way.

This new definition of friendship rocked Simon's understanding, and another realization hit him. Though he didn't think often about it, people knew his story. The villagers of Bethany and the leaders of Jerusalem knew that Simon had been healed of leprosy.

They still called him Simon the Leper.

It was a name Simon didn't care for. He wanted his name to reflect who he was today, not the putrid, rotting person he'd been in the leper colony. But now . . . now Simon felt a sense of joy at the title. If he was Simon the Leper then everywhere he went, every time he left home, people would see the obvious.

Simon the Leper wasn't a leper anymore. He was healed. His life was being used to bring glory to God.

Just as the whispered voice of the Lord had promised when Simon was at his most desperate hour. A peaceful thought came over him. The religious leaders certainly would come to understand the truth about Jesus. Sure, He wasn't the King they were looking for. Politics and governments of this world didn't seem to be His concern.

Jesus was concerned with people.

And He was God. He had proved that much.

The religious leaders would figure out the truth. They had to. They were the keepers of the law. They could check all the prophecies and see that Jesus was the fulfillment. In the meantime, Simon would look forward to his dinner with Jesus.

He smiled to himself. Yes, Jesus would get through these challenging times. No one would harm Him. Not now, anyway. Jesus would share many meals with Simon and their friendship would be long-lasting. Simon would continue to learn from Jesus—not just what it meant to be a follower of God, but something else.

What it meant to be a friend.

## CHAPTER 2

# Martha, the Broken-Hearted

## . . . And Jesus, the Comforting Friend

*Martha wasn't easily given to* panic, but this was different. Her little brother, Lazarus, was sick. So sick the house was beginning to smell of death. Martha should know. She and her sister, Mary, worked every day with dying people.

The fact was, when death crept in through the shadows, it came with a smell.

The smell that now hung near the bed of young Lazarus.

Martha pulled up a chair near her brother's bed. "Lazarus . . . how do you feel?"

He didn't move. Didn't speak.

"Dear brother . . . please talk to me." Martha's words

were a whisper. She touched her hand to his forehead. He was burning up. His skin uncomfortably hot to the touch.

Martha watched him, the way he gasped for each breath even in his sleep. "Lazarus, I'm here. I won't leave you."

They took turns now, she and Mary, so that one of them was always at his side. Lazarus was only sixteen. Strong and handsome. One of the kindest young men in the village. Until he came down with a fever a week ago, Lazarus spent every day helping others.

A sweet memory came to mind. The day Lazarus first started helping the sick in Bethany. "Are you sure you want to do this? They need help at the farms, too."

"I'm sure. I've prayed about it." Lazarus smiled, his eyes bright with love and concern. "Our family has suffered much because of sickness. I will do what I can to make a difference for others in our village."

Lazarus was right. Both Martha's and Mary's husbands had died from the illnesses that plagued Bethany. Usually when people grew ill in Jerusalem, they were sent here. That's what happened to Martha's and Mary's spouses. Once they arrived in Bethany and found a home to share, their husbands grew sicker. Then, a few years ago, the men died—within a week of each other. Now Martha and Mary and Lazarus spent their days caring for the sick in Bethany.

Both sisters were concerned when Lazarus wanted to make a life out of helping people here. But Mary was more at peace with his decision. Even now she was praying in the next room, believing somehow that their brother would be healed.

Martha was more realistic. Lazarus had put himself in danger by helping those with various diseases. And now look. He wasn't getting better.

He was dying.

There was a sound at the door and Martha turned. A smile lifted the weary corners of her mouth as her sister entered the room. "Hi."

Mary looked at Lazarus. "I want to be with him, too." She took the spot on the other side of their brother's bed. "Lazarus, we love you. God is going to make everything better for you. He is."

Martha felt the slightest sense of irritation. Mary's devotion and faith was a beautiful thing. But every now and then she wished her sister would be more in line with the truth. She kept her mouth shut and put her hand alongside her brother's face. "You're not alone, Lazarus. We're here."

They waited, willing Lazarus to move or blink or make a sound. But the only noise was his labored breathing. They could almost hear his heart pounding in his chest, fighting to keep him alive. Mary's eyes filled with sudden hope. "We need to pray." She paused. "Also, I have an idea."

Martha didn't put much stock in Mary's ideas. And though prayer was fine and good, right now they needed medicine. Something to make their brother well again. "What's your idea?"

"Let's send for Jesus."

For a long time Martha let the idea settle inside her. There were a hundred reasons why Mary's plan was pointless. She thought of the kindest way to say so. "Mary, if Jesus is the Savior, then He knows about our brother."

"Yes, but we haven't asked Him to come."

"What's the point?" She felt tears in her eyes. "Lazarus may not have another hour."

"Still . . ." Mary looked almost desperate. She clenched her fists, more determined than usual, more ready to act. "I'm sending for Him. If He comes, our brother will get well."

Martha couldn't argue with that. "Fine." She sighed. "Send for Him."

After Mary left, it occurred to Martha that she'd doubted their friend Jesus. He had spent countless afternoons and evenings with them. He was fond of Lazarus, fond of the work the three of them were doing to help the sick. Martha had absolutely believed Jesus was the Messiah.

Until Lazarus grew ill.

If Jesus was who He claimed to be, then why was their brother dying in the bed beside her? Martha's tears trickled down her cheeks. She felt terrible doubting Jesus, but the evidence of her eyes betrayed her former beliefs. Yes, He had performed miracles in their midst before. But where was He now?

"Lazarus . . . hold on." Martha leaned closer to her brother and whispered the words. "Mary is sending for Jesus." Her tears fell on his face. She wanted to believe it would matter if Jesus came to them. She just didn't know anymore. "Don't die. Please don't die."

Lazarus was the brightest light in their lives. He never tired of doing good, and he tried to be like Jesus for the people of Bethany. After losing their own parents, all three siblings had developed a compassion born of sorrow. Especially Lazarus.

In the evenings when their work was done, Lazarus helped cook and clean. He was quick-witted and kind. When Martha and Mary were tired from the day's duties he would order them to sit down and then he'd take over. He did it without thinking. Lazarus could've been focused on starting a family of his own, but instead he stayed with his sisters. "I'll take care of everything," he would tell them.

Lazarus loved them. He was the sunshine of their lives, and now . . . Martha sniffed and tried to contain the sorrow building in her heart. "Lazarus . . . can you hear me?"

Nothing.

A few hours later Mary joined her again. Martha hadn't eaten or drank water or moved from her spot. "Did you do it?" She searched Mary's face.

Light shone in Mary's eyes. "Yes. I sent word. Jesus will know of our request by tomorrow morning."

Martha looked at Lazarus. She doubted seriously that their brother had that long. But she didn't want to say so. What if he could hear them? Instead she nodded. "I pray He gets here quickly."

With that, Martha left the room. She drank a cup of water and walked straight past the bread on the table. She wasn't hungry. She hadn't been for days. Slowly Martha dropped to the chair at the table and she hung her head. Despite her doubts she cried out to God from the terrified depths of her heart: *God, please don't take him. He's so young. Everyone in the village loves him.* She felt weary, and for the first time her words didn't seem to go anywhere. As if God had turned His back on them.

When she finished praying she hurried back to the bedroom. Mary still had that peaceful look, the one that said she didn't doubt, didn't waver in believing that somehow Jesus would help their brother.

"You go eat." Martha returned to her place by the bed.

"No. I'm fine." Mary took hold of their brother's hand. "I want to be here."

It was only then that Martha noticed something different with Lazarus. His breathing was slower. A stillness had come over him. Martha touched his hand and fear grabbed at her, choking her. "He's . . . worse." She looked closer and put her hand to his head. The fever was gone, but now his skin felt cold. Too cold. Panic filled her heart. "Mary, we're losing him."

"No." Mary's voice held a peace that seemed strangely out of place. "He's getting better."

Martha wanted to scream at her. They'd worked around enough sick people to know the signs. When people were dying, they grew quieter, their breathing more shallow and slower, their skin cold.

The way Lazarus was right now.

She reached for his other hand. "Lazarus, wake up! We're here!"

They watched him take ten more slow breaths and then—in the most awful moment Martha could imagine— Lazarus stopped breathing.

"Lazarus?" Mary's tone was calm, quiet.

"Wake up!" Martha screamed the words. "No, God! Not Lazarus! Please, don't take him." She couldn't breathe, couldn't think. In a rush she covered Lazarus with her own body. "Lazarus, I love you. Please come back to us!"

But Lazarus was still. He was gone. Dead. He had lost the fight.

Mary released his hand and moved to a corner of the room. She slid down along the wall and buried her face in her hands. Though she barely whispered her prayer, Martha could hear her.

"It's too late!" Martha shouted at her. "He's gone. Can't you see?" Angry tears flooded Martha's eyes and she allowed the sobs to wash over her. How could this happen? If Jesus loved them so much, why wasn't He here? She had seen Him perform so many miracles. Why wouldn't He have come when Lazarus first got sick? He could have healed Lazarus then and none of this would've happened. Lazarus would still be alive. Still working and smiling and laughing. Surely Jesus would've known that Lazarus was sick. Jesus said He knew all things. She was absolutely sure of that.

Mary remained silent, her face in her hands.

Martha put her hands on either side of her brother's face. "Lazarus!" She cried out his name between sobs and took him in her arms. His lifeless body was cold, but she held him, rocked him. He was their best friend, the brightest light.

How could he be gone?

Finally Martha could do nothing but gently lay his body back on the bed. A gray tint had come over his face and lips. His skin looked different, lifeless. His body was growing stiff.

In the corner, Mary was crying softly. Martha couldn't take another moment. They should've tried harder to find medicine. Right when he first got sick, they should've gone into Jerusalem and found a doctor who could help him. Why had they waited?

Martha left the room and stepped outside the house. Friends had gathered there, and they looked at her, questions in their eyes. One of them stepped up. "Is he . . . ?"

Fresh tears ran down Martha's face. "Yes." She ran into the arms of the friend. "He's gone. Our dear brother is dead."

All of them began to wail and cry out. Several ran off to get others. Lazarus was dearly loved in the village. He would have the very best funeral. People in Bethany would hear their loud mourning and know the impor-tance of the one who had died. His friends would see to that.

The preparations happened quickly. Even before Martha had time to process what was happening, the body of Lazarus was carried to a tomb on the edge of town. And the wailing throughout Bethany was like nothing any of them had heard.

Martha felt dead inside.

*After several days Martha* found Mary praying at their table.

"What are you praying for?" Martha didn't want to be unkind. But she didn't understand her sister.

Mary looked up. Her eyes were marked by sadness, of course, but she didn't look worried or concerned. There was no denying the hope that remained deep inside her. "I'm asking for God's will. He is not finished with us, Martha."

Martha didn't say it out loud, but she had to wonder. What if God didn't exist at all? What if Jesus was just a nice man with special powers? Certainly if Jesus was God Almighty, the Savior who was to come . . . then He would've come to their house and saved Lazarus.

By now Jesus would've known of their urgent request for several days, and still He hadn't come. How could Mary still believe? Even in their mourning Jesus was nowhere to be found.

Martha was about to head back outside when there was a fierce knock at the door. "Hurry!" someone shouted. "Open up!"

Concern slammed at Martha. What had happened now? Was someone else dying? Another young person? One more volunteer from among the sick? She rushed to the door and opened it, and there stood a group of their friends from the village. "Jesus is coming! He and His followers are almost here!"

Martha blinked, unmoving. *Jesus.* She kept her bitter thoughts to herself. "Thank you."

The people didn't linger at the door. Instead they hurried off toward the edge of town, clearly intent on greeting Jesus when He arrived.

Martha turned to Mary. "Are you going?"

"To meet Jesus?" Mary looked calm, serene.

"Yes. You heard them. He's entering the village." Martha waited.

Mary shook her head. "No. I'll stay here. There's no rush."

She was right about that. Lazarus was dead and lying in a sealed tomb. Martha thought about the situation for a minute and a determination welled within her. She had to go meet Jesus. She had to look Him in the eyes and let Him know personally that Lazarus was dead. Though Jesus could've come sooner and stopped the tragedy from happening, it was too late. She had to be there to put the question forward—spoken or not. What sort of friend didn't come right away?

Martha's disappointment grew as she left the house and headed for the outskirts of Bethany. She saw the crowd first. Of course. There was always a crowd wherever Jesus was. But after losing Lazarus without so much as a word from Jesus, Martha struggled to understand why the crowds followed Him at all.

She pushed and jostled her way past her fellow towns-people until finally, breathless, she stood face to face with Jesus. For a moment their eyes met and held. The com-passion in His expression brought an almost physical comfort. Even so, Martha was angry. Heartbroken.

Slowly, she took a step forward. As she did, the strang-est thing happened. Something she could never have ex-pected. Without any reason or logic, as she approached Jesus, as she looked into His eyes, her anger simply fell away. Vanished. Instead, she was filled with an impossible hope. The kind that had eluded her even before the death of Lazarus.

Martha found her voice. "Lord . . . if You had been here, my brother would not have died." She came closer still. She could no longer sense the crowd, no longer hear their cries for His attention. In all the world there seemed to be only the two of them and this strange, unexplainable thread of hope that bound them together.

Martha and Jesus.

She took another step toward Jesus. Hope swelled within her. "But I know"—every word felt deliberate, intentional—"that even now God will give You whatever You ask."

Jesus searched her eyes, His attention fully hers. "Your brother will rise again."

Her hope waned slightly. "I know he will rise again in the resurrection at the last day."

Again Jesus kept His eyes locked on hers. "I am the resurrection and the life. All who believe in Me will live, even though they die; and whoever lives by believing in Me will never die." He paused, an intensity in His gaze. As if He knew every doubt Martha had ever entertained. His voice fell a notch, His message directed straight to her soul. "Do you believe this?"

Martha felt her knees grow weak. This was no ordinary friend who had disappointed them. This was God in the flesh. Suddenly Martha had no doubt. She bent her head and cried out. "Yes, Lord! I believe that You are the Messiah, the Son of God, who is to come into the world."

Jesus remained, unmoving. His eyes full of love and peace. "Go get Mary."

"Yes, Jesus." Martha turned and ran back to their house. Whatever was happening, Jesus was in control. That much was certain now. She burst through the front door and found Mary where she had left her. This time Mary wasn't alone. Many from the village had come to comfort her.

The house fell quiet as Martha stepped inside. She looked at Mary, breathless from her run. Her sister was crying, harder than ever before. As if the reality of losing Lazarus was just hitting her. Martha calmed down enough to talk. "The Teacher is here. He is asking for you."

Mary didn't often move quickly, but now she rose to her feet immediately. "He asked for me?"

"Yes." Martha started back for the door. "Hurry!"

"Do you think He might . . ." Mary grabbed her cloak, her eyes suddenly wide.

"I'm not sure." Martha felt frantic. "I just know He's the answer."

Together the sisters ran back to the edge of town where Jesus was waiting. The crowd of friends and mourners who had been with Mary ran behind them.

When they made their way through the crowd to Jesus, Mary stepped closer, fell to the ground and started weeping. "Lord . . ." Her cry rang through the air. "If You had been here, my brother would not have died."

She buried her face in her hands, lying in a heap at the feet of Jesus. Her cries were heartbreaking, and around them many people wiped tears from their cheeks. The loss of Lazarus was one of the hardest their town had suffered. Now, the aching, broken heart of Mary—the one always hopeful, always believing—only underlined the sorrow that consumed them all. The combination of losing Lazarus and seeing Mary this hopeless was more than anyone could bear.

Martha joined the others in looking to Jesus. How would He respond now, surrounded by those so broken-hearted? Then something happened that Martha had never seen before. The Teacher's eyes filled with tears. He looked overcome with sadness—the same as the townspeople of

Bethany. Jesus blinked a few times and took a deep breath. He put His hand on Mary's shoulder. "Mary . . ."

She looked up, tears streaming down her face. "Yes, Lord."

"Where have you laid him?"

Mary stood and motioned. "Come and see."

The crowd began moving toward the tomb where Lazarus was buried, but Jesus remained, as if He were frozen in place. Martha and Mary and the disciples, along with many others watched Him as He hung His head for a long moment. Then He lifted His face to heaven and wept. Tears flooded His eyes and spilled onto His cheeks, and though He stood strong, His shoulders set, His body shook with sobs.

This was their friend, Jesus. Savior and God. But friend, too. The One who would come even when it was too late. The One who would weep with them. Martha and Mary cried, too.

Deep inside, Martha understood. Simon had explained it to her when he first visited them. This was not God's plan for His people. He had planned life and abundance and blessing. But because Adam sinned, death and destruction had come into the world. People were killed in violent ways. They suffered at the hands of each other and they died in accidents. And sometimes they got sick and death claimed victory.

For a people God never intended to die.

The sobs washed over their friend and Savior. He

cared. He cared more than Martha ever imagined. He wasn't just busy and callous. He loved Lazarus like He loved Martha and Mary and the other people of Bethany. And this—the death of Lazarus—grieved Jesus in a way they had not seen before.

The pain and loss of death broke His heart.

It was a sight Martha knew she would remember till the day she died. Jesus. Standing with them. Weeping.

The people gathered around had stopped their trek to the tomb. Instead they drew close again, watching Jesus and whispering among themselves, "See how He loved him."

But even then, Martha heard a few of them share their frustrations. "Could not He who opened the eyes of the blind man have kept this man from dying?"

Martha had harbored the same question. But not anymore. Whatever happened next, she believed in Jesus. She would never doubt Him again. Life on earth was not the end of the story, not for her and not for Lazarus. The Scriptures said death would be defeated. That meant one day they would see Lazarus again. They would hear his voice and share conversations with him and sit with him at a meal.

Jesus wiped His hands across His cheeks. His face became set with deep compassion. "Show me where he is." Jesus nodded to Martha and Mary. Then He followed them to the tomb of Lazarus. Standing tall with his shoulders squared, Jesus stared in the direction of the tomb, at the heavy rock sealing the entrance. As if He were staring death in the face. And with a voice rich with authority, He said, "Take away the stone."

Martha was standing closest to Him. She saw the confused looks on the faces of her friends, so she leaned close. "But, Lord . . ." She kept her voice quiet. "By this time there is a bad odor, for he has been there four days."

Immediately Jesus turned to her. The power in His eyes took her breath. "Did I not tell you that if you believe, you will see the glory of God?"

Martha remembered to exhale. She nodded, finally looking from Jesus to the men gathered there. "You heard Him." She motioned toward the entrance of the tomb. "Move the stone."

Only the slightest hesitation followed. Then six men quickly hurried over and rolled the stone from the mouth of the tomb. Silence hung over the crowd. A sense of breathlessness and anticipation overcame them.

Jesus looked up. His eyes still red from crying, He called out, "Father, I thank You that You have heard me. I knew that You always hear me, but I said this for the benefit of the people standing here, that they may believe that You sent me."

The crowd gasped in awe. Some people began shaking. No one said a word. Martha linked arms with Mary, the two of them holding each other up. All eyes were on Jesus.

With that He raised His voice and stared at the open tomb. "Lazarus, come out!"

One minute became two, and the whole time Jesus only looked at the tomb. Martha trembled, her knees weak. She felt light-headed and dizzy. Could it really happen? Would they see their brother again right here? Right now? The very ground felt holy while they waited.

Suddenly a sound came from inside the tomb and a figure appeared. Wrapped in strips of linen with a cloth around his face. He had the walk and step of a young person in good health.

All around Martha people began screaming and dropping to their knees. How could this be? But Martha and Mary only looked at Jesus. Of course He could do this. He could do whatever He wanted. She turned her eyes back to the figure walking from the tomb.

Jesus looked at Martha and Mary and smiled. The smile of their friend. The one they had spent so many meals and afternoons with. He had fresh tears in His eyes, but He chuckled lightly as if to say, *Well . . . what are you waiting for?*

"Jesus?" Martha was the first to speak.

Again He smiled. "Take off the graveclothes and let him go."

Martha and Mary ran to their brother. Moving as quickly as they could they stripped away the cloth from his face and shoulders, and immediately they knew it was true. "Lazarus!" Martha pulled him into her arms. "Dear brother, you're alive!"

Mary took hold of his hand. "How do you feel?"

"Wonderful." Lazarus laughed, slightly confused. He

looked at Jesus and then the linen cloths at his ankles. "What happened?"

Martha breathed in the smell of life; she kissed her brother's cheek and ran her hand along his arm. "You're alive! Thank God, you're alive!"

The crowd stood by in silent wonder, and Jesus approached them. For the longest time He stood nearby while the three siblings clung to each other. It was more than Martha had dared believe. But it had happened right before her very eyes. Her brother who had been dead, was alive. Jesus had commanded death to flee. And death had obeyed.

Yes, it was heartbreaking. Death always would be. But their friend Jesus loved them enough to be here. Enough to stare death in the face and demand life have the final word.

Martha clung to Lazarus. She understood better now. Jesus was not only the One who would cry with them in death and rejoice with them in life.

Jesus was God. Period. No one else had power over death. And since God was love, Jesus was more than Lord and Savior. Messiah. Emmanuel.

He was also the most loving friend they would ever have.

*Two days later, Martha* was making dinner for the friends still gathered, still celebrating the life of Lazarus, when a few of the followers of Jesus came to her. One of them stepped forward. "We want to tell you what happened after you sent for Jesus."

Martha set down the dough she was kneading and leaned against the wall near the oven. "Mary sent for Him." She hesitated. "He took a long time coming." She smiled, curious. None of that mattered now. They had Lazarus. But still . . . "Tell me what happened."

The woman nodded. "One of your friends came running up to Jesus. We all knew whatever had happened, the situation was urgent." She paused. "The person said, 'Lord, the one You love is sick.'"

Martha thought about those days. How Lazarus had died the very night Mary sent for Jesus. And how it had seemed like Jesus did not care to respond. "Go on."

"We all looked to Jesus. The messenger explained that Lazarus was dying. But Jesus did not waver. He didn't look worried. He simply said, 'This sickness will not end in death.'"

"He said that?" Martha felt chills run down her arms. The joy of certainty came over her. "Of course He said that." She shook her head, a smile lifting her lips. "He knew what was to come."

"Yes." The woman grinned. "Jesus also said that your brother's sickness was for God's glory so that," she paused, her tone reverent, "so that God's Son may be glorified through it."

Martha felt a holy sense of wonder. God's Son. That was Jesus, of course. Everything that had happened with Lazarus was to bring glory to Jesus. So that people might know that Jesus had power over death—a power only God could have. It all made sense.

"And so the Son is glorified." Martha's words were barely a whisper. The realization was more than she could truly comprehend. She locked eyes with the woman again. "Did He say anything else? Jesus?"

The woman nodded. She seemed drawn back to that time, to the days before Jesus returned to Bethany. "It wasn't so much what He said but how He responded. We all know how much Jesus loves you and your family. Yet He stayed where He was two more days, healing the sick, teaching about the ways of the Kingdom."

This was the hardest part of the story for Martha. Those days had been the most gut-wrenching for her and Mary. Death had surrounded them and filled their home. Martha's heart felt empty, as if she had died right alongside Lazarus. Martha had been wracked by every emotion—even anger. And during those terrible days their brother died and was buried. All the while they weren't sure if Jesus had even gotten word. Martha would remember forever the terrible pain of desperation and loneliness she felt then. And all the while Jesus intentionally stayed away.

The woman went on. "After two days we followed Jesus back here. Some of the followers warned Him that the people of Judea wanted to stone Him. But Jesus was not afraid. He had a purpose and He explained it to us— but not in a way we understood."

"What did He say?" Martha was gripped by the story,

picturing Jesus headed to Bethany despite the dangers in the journey.

"He said Lazarus had fallen asleep and He needed to go . . . so He could wake him."

"Asleep?"

"Yes." She sighed. "We figured that meant Lazarus was getting better. Sleep was good. But then Jesus spoke again, only this time He looked right at us and said, 'Lazarus is dead.'"

"So He knew?" Martha felt confused again. But then slowly a realization came over her. "He knew. He was going to raise Lazarus from the dead. He had known all the while."

"Yes! Exactly!" The woman's tone grew more excited. "Jesus said He was glad He hadn't been here in Bethany for one reason." She hesitated. "So that all of us might believe."

Martha felt the enormity of the situation. "This was for God . . . to bring glory to Jesus. To prove that Jesus is God with us. The One to come."

The woman's eyes were warm with understanding. "Right. I had to tell you. So you'd know why He didn't come right away."

"It was all part of His plan." Martha's heart overflowed with peace. "Thank you."

"Of course." The woman stood there, not speaking for a moment. Her eyes grew troubled. "There is one more thing."

Martha waited, listening.

"Jesus is in trouble. We've heard from the religious leaders in Jerusalem. They want to arrest Him. There's talk of Him being executed."

"What?" Martha felt the blood drain from her face, felt the rush of adrenaline and fear and horror all at once. "Jesus is the Healer. He is a friend to all." Her heart pounded at the terrible news. "Why . . . why would anyone want to kill Him?"

The woman shook her head. "They don't believe Him. They don't think He's the one the prophets foretold. They are waiting for someone . . . very different."

"So they want to kill Him?" Tears blurred Martha's eyes. "That's ridiculous."

"I know. We all feel that way." The woman's eyes filled with sorrow. "Just pray. Pray as often as you can. Jesus will need our support."

"I will." Martha felt her determination double. "I'll tell Mary and Lazarus, too. We'll stand by Jesus till the end!"

The woman looked nervous, like she wasn't sure how to explain this next part. "The religious leaders have said they may arrest anyone who harbors Jesus. Anyone who cares for Him or offers Him food and shelter. We're all at risk."

"That's fine." Martha didn't hesitate. "Jesus showed us what it means to be a friend. We will stay by Him. Whatever the cost."

"I thought you'd say that."

"Yes." Martha thanked her for the talk. "You've brought much clarity to these recent days."

The woman hugged Martha. "I need to go. Jesus is moving on from here—at least for a short time."

"Okay." Martha held on to the woman's hands for a few seconds. "Tell Jesus something for me. Tell Him Simon the Leper is still looking forward to sharing dinner with Him. When that happens, Mary and Lazarus and I will be there, also. No matter what risk is involved."

The woman's eyes lit up. "I'll tell Him." She smiled as she left. "See you soon."

When the woman was gone, Martha picked up the bread dough and began kneading it again. She could spend a lifetime thinking on all the woman had said and still she would never completely grasp it. How could she ever have doubted Him?

Then something occurred to Martha. Something she'd never considered before. Somewhere deep inside she must've doubted Jesus even before Lazarus grew ill. Otherwise she wouldn't have abandoned her faith in Him so quickly. Crisis had revealed her true feelings.

That had to be it.

And when Jesus came along after her brother's death, when He looked into her eyes and asked if she believed, she was forced to take a stand. Forced to give an answer she would hold on to in good times and bad. And in that awful moment—with Lazarus buried in a tomb and Jesus looking straight into her soul—she had her answer.

She believed Him. She would never doubt Jesus again.

Martha leaned against the wall of her empty kitchen

and a warmth spread through her. God had used the death of Lazarus to glorify Jesus. Not just for His followers or for the religious leaders. Not just for all of Israel and all people yet to come.

But for her personally.

The very darkest days of her life had made her stronger.

She thought again of the things the woman had said about the religious leaders wanting to kill Jesus. She was more determined than ever. She would lay down her own life before she'd let anyone harm Him. As long as she lived, she would stand by Him. She and Mary and Lazarus. All of them.

Jesus was their Savior and Master. But He was also their friend.

If anything happened to Him, they would be there. They would weep, the way Jesus wept at the death of Lazarus. If the day came for grieving, they would grieve together.

Because that's what friends do.

*The dinner plans for* today were set. Martha smiled when she pictured again the reaction from Simon the Leper when he learned that Jesus was coming back through town. Martha had received word from the followers of Jesus that He would be here before the Passover. He wanted to eat at Simon's house!

The meal would be a send-off as Jesus returned to Jerusalem for the holiday.

Even now as she prepared a pot of root vegetables for the dinner, she remembered how happy Simon had been at the news. He had greeted her at the door. "Martha! My dear, how are you?"

"Well." She had felt the way her eyes lit up. "I have good news!" She didn't wait for Simon to respond. "Jesus will pass through Bethany before Passover and He's requested a meal at your house!"

Simon wasn't only happy at the news. Tears filled his eyes. "I've been waiting for this. For the chance to . . ." His voice broke. "To be a friend to Him. After all He's done for me."

"Now it's going to happen."

A smile spread across Simon's handsome face. "I'll be ready."

Since then Martha had remained especially happy for Simon. Leprosy was the worst of all diseases. For most lepers, death was a welcome outcome. Far better than living.

Simon was living proof—as was Lazarus—of the goodness of God and the certainty of the claims of Jesus. Martha smiled as she stirred the pot of vegetables. No matter what came next, there were many people who loved Jesus. Who couldn't wait to spend time with Him.

Finally the time came for the dinner. Martha and Mary and Lazarus walked together to Simon's house. They brought the vegetables and bread and a jug of water. Other people were bringing additional dishes, and Simon had prepared a fatted calf for the occasion.

A sense of celebration had come over all of Bethany.

An hour later, with everything prepared and the table set, Jesus arrived. He brought His twelve disciples along with several who traveled with Him. Even the woman who had shared the story with Martha was there, and a few people Martha didn't expect. One of them was a sinful woman with a past that made most people look the other way.

Martha hesitated as she let the woman inside the house. *Why would Jesus invite her?* she wondered. *Strange choice.* Still, Martha offered her a glass of water. Martha exchanged several glances with Simon about the woman's presence.

Finally Simon pulled Martha aside. "Why is *she* here?" He looked troubled. "I wanted this dinner to be perfect."

"Jesus invited her." Martha had to agree with Simon. This was a celebration of their friend, their Savior. The woman in the next room had lived contrary to the Law of Moses. Martha looked past Simon to the next room. "I guess you'd have to ask Him."

Simon sighed. "Never mind. I just wish . . . I didn't want people like *her* here. Not tonight."

"I know." Martha put her hand on his shoulder. "I understand. Maybe Jesus will explain it later."

Before dinner was served, the entire party gathered in one room. Jesus was resting against one wall when the sinful woman came to Him. She took an alabaster jar of expensive perfume from her cloak and poured it on Jesus's feet. Something Mary herself had done before to honor Jesus.

But this time, an audible gasp came from several in the room—especially from the disciple Judas. He looked indignant. "That woman has just wasted that perfume! It could've been sold to feed the poor for a very long time."

Martha looked around the room. She had to agree. Her eyes met Simon's and she could tell he felt the same way. He raised his chin, clearly indignant, and watched the scene playing out.

Jesus looked sharply at Judas. "Why are you bothering this woman? She has done a beautiful thing to Me. The poor you will always have with you, but you will not always have Me." He looked at the sinful woman. "When she poured this perfume on My body, she did it to prepare Me for burial. Truly I tell you wherever this gospel is preached throughout the world, what she has done will also be told, in memory of her."

The woman began to cry. She hung her head and wouldn't look up. Not at anyone. Her cheeks were deep red and her shoulders trembled. Her shame and painful past were clearly too much for her. Gradually her tears mixed with the perfume on Jesus's feet. Then the woman did something even more outrageous. She used her long dark hair to rub the perfume into Jesus's feet.

Martha stared at her. Whatever the woman had done, she was obviously sorry. Deeply sorry. Martha had to admit it took courage for this woman to join the dinner party, for her to sit in a houseful of judgmental people—

even hostile people. Courage or extreme gratitude. The woman didn't care what anyone thought about her. If it took all she had, she wanted to make things right with Jesus. Even so, Martha could feel the disdain from the others. In light of the comment by Judas, an uncomfortable silence fell over the room and now everything seemed awkward. The tension was terrible.

Finally Jesus looked straight at Simon. His tone was kind, but stern. "I know what you're thinking, Simon. You're thinking if only I knew who was touching me and what kind of woman she was . . ." He paused, his gaze never wavering. "Right, Simon?"

Martha watched as Simon struggled, clearly embarrassed. "My Lord . . . I'm not sure if . . ." He paused.

"Simon." Jesus's tone was still kind, still patient. "I have something to tell you."

The tension in the room grew. No one had expected this to be anything but a joyful meal together. A party. A celebration. Martha could still see the excitement in Simon's face leading up to this day. It was all he'd talked about. But now . . . now Simon looked like he might collapse under the weight of his embarrassment.

Jesus sat up straighter and looked at the faces in the room. Then His eyes turned to Simon again. "Two people owed money to a certain moneylender." The story came slowly, every word full of impact. "One owed him five hundred denarii, and the other fifty. Neither of them had the money to pay him back, so he forgave the debts of both." Jesus paused, letting the story settle into their hearts. "Now . . . which of them will love him more?"

The question was directed at Simon. His answer came immediately. "I suppose the one who had the bigger debt forgiven."

Jesus looked at the sinful woman and then back at Simon. "You have judged correctly." Again He looked at the woman, still holding the empty alabaster jar, still cowering under the critical gaze of the friends of Jesus. When His eyes found Simon again, the compassion in Jesus's expression was enough to make Martha cry.

"Simon, do you see this woman?" Jesus spoke with the kindness of a father. "I came into your house and you did not give Me any water for My feet."

"What?" Simon couldn't believe it. In his rush to make a perfect dinner for Jesus he had forgotten something that important? "I'm sorry, Lord. I'm so sorry."

"I forgive you." He looked at the woman and back at Simon. "But she wet My feet with her tears and wiped them with her hair. You did not give me a kiss, but this woman, from the time I entered, has not stopped kissing My feet. You did not put oil on My head, but she has poured perfume on My feet."

Simon looked horrified. His cheeks grew red and blotchy and his hands shook. He hung his head much like the woman had moments ago. Martha could only imagine what he was feeling. How could Simon have missed all those important moments? She shuddered at the thought of his regret.

Jesus continued. "Therefore, I tell you, her many sins have been forgiven—as her great love has shown. But whoever has been forgiven little, loves little." Jesus drew a deep breath and turned to the sinful woman. "Your sins are forgiven."

A murmur rose from the crowd gathered at Simon's house. "Who is this man who even forgives sins?" one of them whispered.

Martha could feel the dinner getting out of control. The sinful woman gathered her things. She had started this tension—though she probably hadn't meant to. Now she clearly knew no one wanted her there.

Only Jesus.

And then there was Simon, sitting in the corner of the room, his head in his hands. Most of the dinner guests were whispering among themselves, pointing at the woman with the empty alabaster jar . . . or at Simon.

Jesus ignored the whispers. He smiled at the woman. "Your faith has saved you . . . Go in peace."

Once more the woman bowed toward Jesus, her gratitude exuding from her like a tangible force. "Thank You, Master." She shook her head, as if there were no words to fully express how she felt. Her cheeks weren't red any longer and peace filled her eyes. She took a few steps toward the door and turned to Jesus once more. "You are the Messiah."

Everyone in the room grew silent. As if a holy wonder had come over them all. So many people still did not truly understand Jesus. They didn't know or believe that He was God.

But now He at least had their attention.

*Dinner wasn't the same* after that. Some guests returned to their whispers, others stayed silent. The feeling of joy and celebration was gone and in its place a sober sense of understanding for some. Confusion for others. Quiet angry debate broke out even among the disciples of Jesus. Whether the woman should've used the expensive perfume and whether Simon and the rest were justified in thinking she shouldn't have walked through the door today.

Simon stood and cleared the table. He brought Jesus a basin of water and washed His feet and did the same for the disciples. Martha sat next to Mary and Lazarus, the three of them watching Simon.

Finally Martha stood and followed Simon to the sink. The dishes were cleared and he was about to start washing them. His face was long, forlorn.

"Simon . . . I'm sorry. That was difficult."

He lifted his eyes and shook his head. "I missed it, Martha. I wanted Jesus here so badly. I wanted to impress Him, show Him how much I cared." He stared at the dishes in his hands. "I got caught up in the details, and I forgot about who He was." His shoulders fell. "Dishes? Compared with greeting the Master?"

Simon looked back at Jesus in the other room. "How could I have forgotten to give Him a cup of water? Something so small?"

"It's okay." Martha put her hand on Simon's shoulder. "The Teacher understands."

"No." Simon shook his head, refusing to accept what he'd done. "I had one chance to be a friend to Him and I failed. I was distracted. I couldn't see past that woman in my house." His eyes narrowed, as if he were seeing the scene play out again. "Now . . . because of Jesus, I can see it all. None of us deserve forgiveness."

Martha had never asked Simon his story, about his days as a leper. "What was it like . . . before Jesus healed you?"

Simon leaned against the wall and the story seemed to mix with the tears in his eyes until finally he found his voice. "I was perfect. A Pharisee." He looked at Martha, the memories clearly alive again. "And then overnight I became a leper. An outcast. Unclean." He exhaled. "But still . . . I really thought I'd done nothing wrong."

Martha listened while Simon explained again how Jesus had healed him. "But I must have thought very little of that healing. Because here"—he motioned toward the other room—"with Jesus in my house, I didn't even remember to properly greet Him." He waited, clearly caught up in the details. "But that woman . . . she knew the magnitude of forgiveness."

"We are all sinners." Martha's voice was quiet. Kind,

the way Jesus had demonstrated earlier. "Maybe that's the lesson."

"Me worst of all." He brought his hand to his face and covered his eyes for a moment. "I'm a prideful man. Arrogant. Like the Pharisee I once was, today I was too caught up in throwing a good dinner to see God working a miracle in that woman's life in the next room."

Martha smiled. "If it makes you feel better, I've done the same thing." She breathed deeply. "It takes time and intention to sit at the Master's feet. To notice all He has to offer us."

"Time." Simon looked out at Jesus, still talking to the other dinner guests. "That's what makes someone a friend of Jesus. The time we give Him." He looked at Martha. "I won't forget that. I've been forgiven even more than the woman with the perfume. Far more."

Martha nodded. "In our own way, we each have. Jesus offers life. None of us needs a little forgiveness or more of it. We are all equally undeserving."

For a long while they stood there, watching Jesus teach the others, studying his patient ways and gentle tone. Martha looked at the dishes in Simon's hand. "Set them down, Simon. The dishes can wait."

Time with Jesus could not.

Then, in deeper understanding of all they'd been given that day, Simon and Martha returned to the room and sat near the feet of Jesus. Martha felt more convinced than ever that she'd been right about the depth of love

Jesus had for all of them. As their friend, He would teach them and sit with them, heal them and weep with them. And though Martha didn't want to think about it, she knew something else. If it came down to it in the coming days, He would do something even greater.

He would die for them.

## CHAPTER 3

# Jairus, the Two-Faced Leader

## ... And Jesus, the Loyal Friend

*J*airus was beyond frustrated.

Jesus was causing more trouble than the religious leaders could handle. The healings had continued—even after they ordered Simon out of Jerusalem to Bethany. No matter what they did, word about the miracles of Jesus continued to spread.

It was time to do something about the situation. Time to stop the man they called Master. People had left the Temple to follow Jesus, Temple dues were going unpaid, and the religious leaders bickered often about what to do next.

The whole city of Jerusalem was divided.

The high priests sat around the table with Jairus at

the center. He folded his hands and looked at the faces staring back at him. "We need to call a meeting of the Sanhedrin." He felt the weight of his position as chief priest of the Temple more than ever before. "The stories of Jesus continue to pour in. Our people are on opposing sides."

At that, a Pharisee named Gamaliel stood. "Forgive me for being so forward." He nodded at Jairus. "I've been thinking about this Jesus."

A chorus of comments followed: "We've all been thinking of Him," and "We can't get away from Him."

Jairus held up his hand, quieting the other priests. He looked at Gamaliel. "Go ahead. Tell us what you've been thinking."

"Thank you." The man was one of the oldest Pharisees, the corners of his eyes lined with the years, his words full of wisdom. "Reports about Jesus are widespread."

"Yes." Jairus wanted him to get to the point. He had Temple duties to complete and he wanted to get home. His little girl had fallen ill and this morning her fever was higher still. He tapped his foot on the floor. "Go ahead."

Gamaliel nodded. "People tell of Jesus giving sight to the blind. We've seen at least one of those right here in this very court. Remember the man's words? He had no idea how or why Jesus healed him. He only knew he was blind and now he can see." Gamaliel looked around, clearly hoping for approval.

Jairus waved his hand in the air. "I think we all re-member that. We determined the man was a fraud, if I'm correct. Not a reliable witness whatsoever."

A doubtful look passed over Gamaliel's face. "He did have witnesses. Even his parents attested to the fact that he had been born blind." The older Pharisee pressed on. "Of course, that was hardly the only report. We've heard of the lame walking, people cured of demonic possession. And a few weeks ago"—he paused—"the teenager in Bethany—Lazarus—was raised from the dead."

That was all Jairus could take. He slammed his hand on the table. "We have no proof of that." The conversation was pointless. His frustration doubled. "These . . . follow-ers of Jesus are a tricky lot. The boy's death might've been staged, for all we know."

"That's just it." Gamaliel remained calm. "We don't know." He looked around the room. "I've done some re-search on my own. Everyone in Bethany says there was no doubt about the death of Lazarus. He had been buried in a tomb for four days when Jesus returned." He stared at Jai-rus. "Four days? If he had been buried alive as part of a plot, he would've suffocated. If indeed he was dead, his body would've been rotting after that much time." Gama-liel shrugged. "The people I've talked to say they watched the stone rolled away from the tomb. They heard Jesus call him out and then, with their own eyes, they saw Lazarus walk from the tomb. He still had the graveclothes on."

A piercing doubt shot through Jairus. He sat back in his chair and gritted his teeth. His eyes locked on to

Gamaliel's and suddenly, for the first time, he considered the impossible. What if . . . what if Jesus really was the . . .

No. The Messiah would be a king. Not a penniless carpenter's son. Jairus waved his hand at the others. "Thoughts on Lazarus? On how that could've happened?"

A discussion broke out and Jairus massaged his brow. The so-called evidence about Jesus was growing like wildfire, surrounding Jairus and the religious leaders on every side.

One of the Sadducees stood and nodded toward Gamaliel. "I'm concerned, also. What if Jesus is telling the truth?" He looked at Jairus. "We all remember Simon, our former friend. He gave Jesus credit for healing his leprosy. And we all know such a healing is impossible without some divine touch."

At the mention of Jesus possibly having a divine touch, three of the Pharisees tore their robes. "Blasphemy! Only God has a divine touch!"

"The law says blasphemy is punishable by death!" Another Pharisee pounded his fist on the table. "We need to apprehend Him and carry out the law. Immediately!"

"Enough!" Jairus stood and motioned for silence. The Sadducee across the table slowly sat down.

Jairus wanted to be firm and certain. He wanted to agree about the arrest of Jesus. But after hearing again about Lazarus, Jairus's conviction wasn't what it had been. In its place a fear began creeping through Jairus. *What if* . . . He couldn't put the thought into words. He felt like a blasphemer even considering the idea. But still . . . the apparent evidence was suffocating him. The older Pharisee was honored by all the people. If he had something to say, Jairus wanted to hear it all.

Jairus dropped to his seat and pointed at Gamaliel. "Finish."

Gamaliel nodded his thanks. "Here's my idea." He held out his hands. "Consider carefully what you intend to do to Jesus." He paused. "Some time ago Theudas appeared, claiming to be somebody, and about four hundred men rallied to him. He was killed and all his followers were dispersed and it came to nothing."

Several people around the table nodded, remembering the situation.

"After him," Gamaliel continued, "Judas the Galilean appeared in the days of the census and led a band of people in revolt. He, too, was killed, and all his followers were scattered."

The stories were only making Jairus more uneasy. He waited, knowing where Gamaliel was headed.

"Therefore," the older Pharisee pleaded with them, "in the present case, I advise you: Leave Jesus alone! Let Him go! For if His purpose or activity is of human origin, it will fail. But if it is from the Father, you will not be able to stop Him. You will only find yourselves fighting against God."

Again one of the Sadducees ripped his robe. "There you go again, Gamaliel. Calling this Teacher 'God.' Are you crazy?"

Gamaliel looked at the man for a long moment. "Time will tell."

Jairus pondered the words of the Pharisee. If Jesus and His teachings, if the reports of healings, were of human origin, then His mission would fail. If only he could see for himself whether Jesus did, indeed, have miraculous powers. If so, Jairus would have to admit that maybe . . . maybe it was possible Jesus was telling the truth. That His claims of being the Messiah were actually true.

Again discussion broke out. Gamaliel sat down and turned his eyes to Jairus, as if to say, *Well, what are you going to do about this?* The debate was growing more sharp. One of the leaders of the Pharisees shouted at the others, "I don't care what the rest of you do, He must be punished for blasphemy. I plan to arrest Jesus and put Him to death."

Across the table, Gamaliel shrugged. "I've told you my thoughts. I'll say them again every time the subject of Jesus and His followers comes up."

All eyes turned to Jairus. He was the chief priest, the leader of the synagogue. He cleared his throat. "It's my opinion that—"

There was a sound at the door and one of the Temple guards burst through. He looked at Jairus. "I'm sorry, sir. I have a message for you. It's urgent."

Jairus felt his heart pound against his chest. He excused himself from the table and stepped out with the guard. "We were in the middle of a very important council. This better be an emergency."

"It is." The guard's expression was etched with concern. "It's your daughter, sir. She is dying. Your wife says she may only have a few hours." He took a step back. "I'm sorry."

The guard left and Jairus was alone. His daughter was dying? "No, God!" He uttered the words through clenched teeth. For twelve years the child had been the light of his life, his greatest joy. "Please, God, no!" He could feel his heart ripping in two. Slowly, he fell to his knees and pressed his face against the earthen floor. "Not my baby, God. Please."

Suddenly he was there again waiting for his wife, the baby just minutes from being born. And the midwife had cried out that something was wrong and Jairus remembered how they had already lost four babies. Four. And this was his wife's last chance for a child.

So Jairus had prayed to God, begging Him that this baby might live. Their only child. Their last attempt at a family. And somehow, despite the crisis at hand, his wife had given birth to a little girl. A precious daughter with eyes like her mother's and cheeks like his own.

And he had held her and rocked her when her mother was too tired to get up in the middle of the night. Sometimes when they were alone, Jairus would sing to her. Little songs of hope and encouragement. Songs that expressed his belief in God and in her and in the goodness of her future.

The years had passed too quickly, and his little girl was two and she was walking everywhere, laughing and giggling, her presence filling their home with joy. And he would come home from a long day at the Temple, home from the arguing and assessing and judging and casting out the sick, and there he'd find his wife and daughter. And his little girl would run into his arms and hug him. Her little hands around his neck.

And she was older. She was seven and easily the brightest girl any in their extended family had ever known. Charming and witty, always smiling. He could hear her voice ringing out. "I love you, Daddy. You're the best father in all the world."

Jairus could hardly believe she was already twelve— on the brink of becoming a young woman. He thanked God every day for the gift of her in their lives. Their only child. Their daughter. Talitha.

And now they only had hours?

Tears stung at his eyes. His heart raced within him, his mind screamed for an answer. His baby was dying and there was nothing he could do about it. "Talitha, hold on, baby. Your father's coming."

Jairus scrambled to his feet. He felt dizzy and sick to his stomach. Hopelessness threatened to suffocate him. His precious Talitha was his home, his heart. His every-thing. *Talitha, don't die. Please, God, no! Not Talitha.* The name wasn't the one given to her at birth. But it was the name Jairus called her. Talitha meant "little girl," and even though she was twelve now, she would always be his baby. His little daughter.

He had to do something. Jairus raced for the side door

of the Temple. He would go to her and hold her and pray over her. He would beg God again for a miracle. Yes, that was the answer. If he hurried he would reach her in time and certainly God would heal his daughter.

After all, he was the synagogue leader.

Normally as he walked through the streets of Jerusalem, Jairus would carry himself in a certain way. Slow and proper, head held high. Between that and the priestly robes he wore, everyone he passed on the street always knew he was someone special. Jairus. Leader of the Temple. Never had Jairus appeared in public without the utmost decorum.

But now tears filled his eyes and he gasped for breath. He didn't care who saw him or what they thought. Nothing mattered except his precious Talitha. He raced out the door and onto the street, wiping at his eyes so he could see. He ran as fast as he could, his robes gathering dust and flapping behind him.

Everyone noticed. He caught their glances and stares, the way they pointed at him. Why was Jairus running like a crazy man through the street? Jairus didn't care. Had any of them ever lost their only daughter? He felt about to pass out, and his breathing came in jagged gasps. None of it mattered.

*Talitha, baby, hold on. Daddy's coming. God, please, spare her. I would do anything if only . . .*

*Anything, Jairus?*

Jairus felt his heart skip a beat. What was that? Who had spoken to him? Suddenly Jairus came to a halt. His chest heaved from the way he'd raced down the street. His arms and legs trembled. He turned one way and then another, frantic to find the face that had said the words.

But there was no one. No one even close. "Who spoke to me, God?" His words were breathy, muffled by the sound of his pounding heart. He lifted his eyes to heaven. "Do you have a message for Your servant?"

Only one word came to mind, but it came as surely as his next breath.

Jesus.

He could run to his house and hold his baby girl, rock her and pray for her and beg God for a miracle. Or . . . Jairus squeezed his eyes shut. *Is this You, God? Are You telling me to go to Jesus?*

This time there was no response, no holy whisper. In a rush of details, Jairus thought of every miracle ever credited to Jesus. Who was he to deny the eyewitness accounts of so many people? Never mind Jewish law or the opinions of all the teachers in the synagogue. They were only people, after all. The proof was in the miracles themselves. And if the miracles were true, then maybe Jesus really was . . . Maybe He might really be . . .

Jairus felt his body collapsing, giving way beneath the flood of possibility and regret. If he didn't finish the run home, he would miss his daughter's final hours. But the truth was, Jairus could not help Talitha. Not if she was that close to death. No medicine would make a difference. And now it seemed God Himself was telling Jairus to turn around and not go home.

But instead to go and find Jesus.

Jairus turned and put one foot in front of the other in the direction opposite his home. Opposite his dying baby girl. His Talitha. This was crazy. He had spent most of the last few years waging war against Jesus. When the one they called Teacher would come to the Temple, Jairus was tolerant. Friendly at times. Jesus probably believed Jairus was His friend. But nothing could be further from the truth. Behind closed doors Jairus was one of the most outspoken against Jesus. He was even considering having Jesus arrested and killed.

But if Jesus could truly heal people, then maybe . . . maybe that was his little girl's only chance. The idea seemed crazy. Jairus could hardly believe he was considering it. Still, in this moment Jairus would've thrown himself off a bridge or laid in front of a galloping horse if it meant saving Talitha. He was beyond desperate.

And what of the voice he'd heard a minute ago? If God wanted Jairus to go to Jesus, then maybe Jesus would help him. Jairus squeezed his eyes shut, still breathing hard. *Is that You, God? Is that what You want from me? That I would run to Jesus in my gravest hour?*

Another sensation came over him as he moved further away from his home. He needed to hurry. His daughter did not have long. He could feel that single truth in the depths of his heart. In the place where she would always live, no matter what happened.

In a rush he picked up his pace. The faster he moved the more certain he became. The blind could see. The lame could walk. The demon-possessed were in their right mind. Simon was healed. Lazarus was alive, healthy and whole.

Whatever terrible things he had believed about Jesus, he'd been wrong. Dead wrong. He felt more sure with every frantic step. Jesus was the Healer. And like Gamaliel said earlier, if Jesus was from heaven, then they could do nothing to stop Him.

And why would they?

To the contrary, it was time to acknowledge that Jesus really was the Messiah He claimed to be. Or if not the Messiah, someone sent by God. Jairus was too confused, too terrified to give his thoughts much order. He raced through the streets, his robes again flying behind him, the cords of his robes tangled at his sides. Dust kicked up and Jairus didn't worry about breathing. He ran as if his daughter's life depended on it.

He had to reach Jesus.

*Please, God! Let me find Jesus in time. He can save my little girl. I believe, Father. I do.*

Jairus wasn't sure his feet would hold out, but he kept running anyway. And finally, as he turned a corner, there was Jesus—surrounded by a crowd a few streets down. Jairus held up his hand as he ran. "Jesus! Jesus, help me!"

His shouts gained the attention of everyone in the crowd. They stopped and turned to him, staring at his disheveled robes and sweaty face. Their eyes grew wide and their mouths hung open. He could read their thoughts.

Was this Jairus, the synagogue leader? The one always so dignified?

Jairus ignored them. "Jesus, please!" he cried out again. The crowd parted and he was able to get through, straight to the place where Jesus stood.

Then Jesus's eyes turned to Jairus, and Jairus saw an unmistakable knowing. As if Jesus knew every wicked, doubting thing that had ever crossed Jairus's mind. His plotting against Jesus and his insincerity in their Temple interactions. Jesus knew it all.

If—as he ran through the streets—Jairus had been somewhat certain that Jesus was the Messiah, he was absolutely convinced now. God had brought him here. Jesus was the answer. The only one who could help his Talitha.

Jairus didn't hesitate. He threw himself to the ground at the feet of Jesus. Gasping for breath, dust covering his face and sticking in his throat, sobs crowding his words, Jairus pleaded with Jesus. "My little daughter is dying. Please come and put Your hands on her so that she will be healed and live." Jairus reached out toward Jesus. "Please, Master!"

At the sight of Jairus facedown before Jesus, at the way Jairus called Jesus Master, a gasp came from those in the crowd nearby. This was the last thing they had expected from a religious leader. Especially now, when the Sadducees and Pharisees had turned on Jesus.

Again, Jairus paid them no heed. He lay on the ground tangled up in his dirty robes and he lifted his eyes to Jesus. "I'm desperate. Please heal her!"

The calm in the Teacher's eyes was otherworldly. Like nothing Jairus had ever experienced. Jesus reached out His hand and helped Jairus to his feet. "Take Me to her."

Jairus could hardly believe it! Jesus was willing! He was going to make Talitha well and all would be right with his world. Tears flooded his eyes. *Hold on, baby. Jesus will make you better!* He struggled to find his voice. "Come on, Jesus. Follow me."

Jairus led the way while Jesus and his followers pressed in behind. But all around them the crowd grew. Hundreds of people called out to Jesus, begging Him for a healing or a chance to be set free from any of a hundred afflictions.

Couldn't the people see Jesus was trying to get somewhere? Jairus wanted to scream at them to back off, get out of the way. His daughter didn't have long. His racing heart urged him to hurry to his little girl, but Jairus had to wait for the Teacher. If only the people would clear a path.

They had barely made any progress when Jesus stopped and looked around. For a moment he scanned the crowd. "Who touched My clothes?"

Jairus wanted to scream. Why was Jesus so concerned about his garments? *Be patient,* he told himself. He didn't want Jesus to change his mind and not come. He watched as the disciples looked at each other and then at Jesus.

"You see the people pushing against You," one of them said. "And yet You can ask, 'Who touched Me?'"

But Jesus refused to take another step. He kept looking around to see who had brushed up against His clothes. And then, a woman came and fell at His feet, as if she couldn't hide the fact another minute.

Jairus narrowed his eyes. Something about the woman looked familiar. He studied her, the profile of her face. And then as she lifted her eyes to Jesus suddenly Jairus knew.

It was the bleeding woman. Jairus had seen her every year for the last twelve years. Each spring she came to the religious leaders and each time they determined she still had her disorder. A disgusting bleeding disorder. And so every spring they turned her away. Cast her out of the Temple, out of the city. Jairus had personally been responsible for banishing her these past twelve years.

Suddenly the number hit him. *Twelve years.* Ever since . . .

He felt his heart drop to his knees. The woman had been bleeding, cast out of the city in disgrace for as long as his precious daughter had been alive. The same twelve years.

Jairus didn't even know the woman's name. He only knew this. No matter what had separated them before, here and now they were on equal ground. Both in dire need of a touch from the Master's healing hand.

Time was slipping by. Many blocks away Jairus's daughter was dying. They needed to hurry. But Jesus didn't seem in a rush. He looked at the woman as if He had all the time in the world. As if time were in His very hands. He urged the woman to explain herself.

And so she did.

With a crowd of hundreds gathered round, the woman told how she had a bleeding disorder and how for twelve long, shameful years she had suffered a great deal under the care of many doctors. But instead of getting better she had gotten worse. Certainly the leaders of the synagogue had done nothing to help her.

Then the woman had heard about Jesus.

It was against the Jewish law for her to even step foot in the city without approval from the religious leaders. And yet she must've known that if she didn't get to Jesus she would die. Her life depended on it. So she had gone against the law and come to Him. The crowds clearly hadn't stopped her.

"I knew that if I just touched the hem of Your garment, I would be healed." Tears streamed down her face as she told Jesus what had happened. "And so I did. I touched your cloak and that very same moment, I was healed. The bleeding stopped!" A few sobs shook her shoulders. "I felt it."

A cry of praise and astonishment went through the crowd. Jesus had healed a woman sick for twelve years. Without a word. Without a touch. His power was that great. Like He had done for Jairus earlier, Jesus helped the woman to her feet.

"Thank You, Jesus!" Tears of joy choked her voice. "I will be forever thankful. You are the Messiah. The Savior."

Jairus watched, amazed. He and his peers had been

quick to cast this woman out of the Temple, quick to declare her worthless. Her life didn't matter to them. But to Jesus, the woman was worthy indeed. He had set her free, right here in a single moment. Shame fell over Jairus. Why hadn't they cared for the woman? Couldn't they have done something to help her?

Then slowly, a compassionate smile lifted Jesus's face. "Daughter, your faith has healed you. Go in peace and be freed from your suffering."

But even while Jesus was speaking the words, Jairus noticed a commotion. Several of the religious leaders from his Temple were approaching. One of them was the Sadducee who had promised to kill Jesus. Three other priests were with him, along with several of Jairus's extended family. The religious leaders were gruff as they came, pushing people out of the way, their eyes on Jairus.

When they reached him they hesitated, looking Jairus up and down. His dirty robes, his tearstained face. The way he clearly had been leading Jesus back to his house, to his little girl. All of it seemed to disgust them. They turned and sneered at Jesus, and then looked back at Jairus again. The Sadducee spoke first. "Your daughter is dead." He spat the words. The Sadducee crossed his arms, almost as if he were satisfied by the outcome. He allowed a single sarcastic laugh as he looked at Jesus. "Why bother the Teacher now?"

Jairus felt the weight of her death like a wagon full of bricks on his chest. "No!" he cried out and again he fell to his knees. "No, God! Not my girl. Please!"

He caught a look of disdain on the faces of his fellow Pharisees and Sadducees. They didn't need to say what they felt. Their expressions said it all. Jairus was a fool. How could he have believed in Jesus? He should've gone to his daughter, not to the one who claimed to be God.

No doubt, Jairus would be banned from his duties as leader of the synagogue for this. He had gone against the prevailing thought and shown a very public allegiance to Jesus. And it had gained him nothing.

The world around Jairus was spinning, his heart shattering. But even when there was no logical reason why, Jairus believed. He believed enough to look up into the eyes of Jesus.

And Jesus was looking straight at him. "Jairus." Once again Jesus helped Jairus to his feet. "Don't be afraid. Just believe."

Believe? Again he wondered if Jesus could read his thoughts. It was the only thing he could express. The one thing that remained after the devastating news of his daughter's death. Jairus still believed.

He nodded and brushed at the sudden tears sliding down his dusty cheeks. "What now, Jesus?"

The Teacher did not waver. "Take Me to her."

She was dead. That's what his friends had told him. But Jesus wanted to see her anyway. Jairus nodded. Was it possible? Did he dare still hope? He didn't know. He wasn't even sure how he managed to put one foot in front of the other. But somehow Jairus led Jesus to his home.

When they were a short distance away, Jesus stopped

and turned to three of His disciples. "Only you three may follow Me."

The crowd began to move as Jesus and Jairus and the three approached the house. Already there was a group of mourners gathered outside. With loud cries and wails they grieved the death of the daughter of Jairus.

It was a moment too great to bear. Jairus hung his head and wept. He was an important figure in Jerusalem. And so the mourners were many—most of them paid as part of the acknowledgment of a life lost. An important life.

The daughter of Jairus.

But even as Jairus wiped at his tears, he heard Jesus raise His voice louder than the mourners. Jairus opened his eyes and looked at the Teacher. Something about His presence conveyed impossible hope. Absolute confidence. At about that time, Jairus saw his wife run from the house to his side. She was overcome with sobs.

"Is she . . ." Jairus couldn't stand to ask the question, but he had to know.

"Jairus . . . she's gone." His wife buried her face in his shoulder. "You weren't here to say goodbye."

It was true. He'd missed out on the final moments of his little girl's life. Jairus put his arm around his wife and held her close. Still, here in the midst of his darkest moment, Jairus believed. He'd done the right thing, going to find Jesus. He believed it with his entire being.

A few feet away, Jesus raised his hand. "Why all this commotion and wailing?"

The crowd of mourners gradually quieted, all eyes on Jesus.

The Master lowered His hand. "The child is not dead, but asleep."

At this pronouncement, the mourners began to chuckle and laugh, until they were uproariously mocking Jesus. "What's He talking about?" some of them yelled. "We saw her dead body ourselves! Does Jesus not know the difference between sleep and death?"

A righteous anger filled Jesus's face. "Leave this place!" His voice boomed above the sound of their laughter, and the crowd became instantly silent.

A few of the mourners still muttered to themselves, but all of them left. And when they were gone, Jesus held out His hand to Jairus and his wife. Then he motioned to His three disciples. "Come. Follow Me."

This time Jesus led the way straight to the quiet, dark room where the child lay, motionless. Void of color or life. Jairus resisted the urge to run to his little girl and take her dead body in his arms. His grief pressed in against him until he could bear it no more.

Before Jairus might collapse beside his daughter's bed, Jesus reached out His hand to her. Jairus could not believe what happened next. As Jesus touched their daughter's fingers, she opened her eyes.

Jairus could see the look of love that came over Jesus. He spoke straight to her. "Talitha, I say to you, get up!"

*Talitha?* Jairus felt the air sucked from the room. How

would Jesus have known his nickname for his daughter? The name was not common at all. And yet . . .

Before Jairus could finish his thought, and with his wife clinging to him, their Talitha immediately stood up. His precious girl—dead a moment before—was now standing! As if she'd never been sick at all.

Jairus sucked in a quick gasp. He leaned against his wife so he wouldn't collapse. "Jesus . . . Master . . . Messiah, thank You! We don't deserve Your kindness!" Jairus put his hand on Jesus's shoulder.

At the same time, Talitha looked first at Jesus and then at her parents. "Mother! Father!" She ran to them and fell into their arms.

In all his life, Jairus had never known a sweeter moment. His daughter was whole and healthy, more alive than ever before.

She stayed there, holding on to her parents. Jairus looked over his wife's shoulder and met the eyes of Jesus. The Master was looking straight at him and again there were no words.

Jesus's expression said more than His words might've conveyed. As if He were saying, *See, Jairus? This is what a true friend is like. . . . You understand?*

Jairus nodded slowly, his eyes never leaving Jesus. He understood. A true friend forgave and remained kind even when there was no reason at all. Jairus had been full of pride and judgment toward the hurting people of the synagogue. The bleeding woman. Simon the Leper.

Especially toward Jesus.

And yet when Jesus had been to the Temple for teaching, Jairus had given the appearance of a friend. Jesus, meanwhile, was a true friend. He pressed on to save Talitha, when He had a right to turn His back.

"Go and get the child something to eat." Jesus patted the girl's head. "You are healed, little one."

Talitha looked at Jesus and grinned. "Thank You, Master."

Then she and her mother moved to the next room. His followers went, too, until only Jairus and Jesus were there, near his daughter's now empty bed.

"This is important, Jairus. See to it that no one knows about this."

Jairus immediately understood. Jesus's miracles were adding up, and the religious leaders were making a plan. A deadly plan. One that Jairus had been at the center of until today. If the Sadducees and Pharisees found out that Jesus had raised the dead daughter of Jairus to life, they would not be able to dismiss it as staged or false. They would be compelled to act. No matter what the wise old Gamaliel said.

He nodded. "Yes, Master. I won't say a word."

Jesus smiled and put His hand on Jairus's shoulder. "Thank you."

"No, Lord . . . thank You. I could never repay You for what You've done."

Jesus smiled once more and then He and His followers left. Jairus watched Him go and he wondered what would happen next, what his future would be. The religious leaders would certainly refuse him his place as leader of the synagogue. The chief priest couldn't be seen begging at the feet of Jesus.

Whatever they did to him, Jairus didn't care. But there was one problem. If he could no longer sit at the table with the top religious leaders, he couldn't convince them that Jesus was the Messiah. He couldn't sway them from arresting Jesus and putting Him to death. The thought made him sick to his stomach. Because there was only one thing he was desperate to do now.

Stand up for Jesus.

The way a true friend would do.

And one more thing. He walked into the next room and for an hour he and his wife talked with Talitha, explaining to her all that had happened. The little girl's eyes were bright with hope and belief.

"Daddy, of course He's the Master. He speaks the words of life every time He walks through the streets of Jerusalem. Didn't you believe Him before?"

Shame threatened to overshadow the joy of his daughter's miraculous healing. "I didn't." He kissed the top of her head. "But I do now. I always will."

"Good." She laughed at something her mother said. "Tell me about the loud mourners again, Mother. I want to see it in my mind."

As his daughter spoke, Jairus remembered something Simon had told them the day he appeared in the Temple free from his leprosy. He said the Teacher had ordained praise from the mouths of children. At the time, Jairus had laughed at the idea. Why would children believe in Jesus?

Now, looking at Talitha, he understood. Children were closer to God. Without the walls of cynicism and jealousy and legalism. Without preconceived ideas and selfish motives, Jesus's validity as Emmanuel was obvious.

Jairus had one more thing to do. Otherwise he couldn't sleep tonight.

He stood and bid his wife and daughter farewell. "I'll return before nightfall."

"Don't go to the Temple, my love." His wife looked concerned. "They may not . . ." She glanced at Talitha, clearly not wanting to upset the child. "Just don't. Please."

"I'm not. It's something else."

The journey took less than an hour, precious time during which Jairus constantly kept his eyes on the blue sky overhead, thanking God for everything about the day. The events played again, the devastating news and the way he had been prompted by God to find Jesus. The slow pace of the crowd and the woman healed by just a touch of the Master's cloak. And finally the way Jesus had pulled Talitha from death.

Indeed, Jesus had stood toe-to-toe with death and He had won. With only a few words. A chill passed over Jairus though it was well after noon and the sun was hot on his shoulders. He set his eyes straight ahead and ten minutes later he reached the house. He knocked at the door and prayed the man on the other side would receive him. Though the man had every reason to spit in his face.

The door opened and there was Simon the Leper. Simon the Pharisee. The one who had been a friend before he fell sick. "Hello, Simon."

Simon took a few steps back. "Go, Jairus. Leave me alone. I won't return to the Temple. I already told you that. I have a life here now and I—"

"Simon." Jairus bowed his head slightly. "I have not come to trouble you again. I have come to apologize."

Simon, his onetime friend, couldn't have looked more surprised if Jairus had sprouted wings and flown away. Simon relaxed his shoulders. "You . . . you what?"

"I've seen Jesus. He is the Master. The Messiah. I know that now."

Simon's mouth hung open, but he stepped back and seemed to find his voice. "Come . . . in, Jairus."

"Thank you." Jairus couldn't imagine going to sleep tonight without making this visit. Once they were inside Jairus looked straight at Simon. "I owe you an apology. I'm so . . . so very sorry." He let his eyes wander along the perfect skin of Simon's arms and face. "Jesus really did heal you. I believe you now."

"Yes." Simon seemed to have caught his breath from the shock. "He healed me with a single touch."

Jairus nodded. He thought of his daughter's healing and joy flooded his soul.

For the next hour the two talked about the Master, how His miracles were widely known by now and how they were real. Simon shared about the dinner at his house and how Jesus had talked of His burial.

"I'm worried about Him." Jairus squinted against the certainty of the dark times ahead. "I wish I could tell the others. But . . ."

"They won't listen." Simon gave a sad smile. "The way you didn't listen to me."

Before it was time for Jairus to leave, he wanted to be clear about one thing. "You and I, we were friends before you got sick." Jairus hesitated. "But not really. I was only willing to be your friend if you were well. If you were perfect, like the rest of us. Like we thought we were. Once your situation changed, once you became less than whole, I turned my back."

Simon waited, listening. His eyes shone with understanding.

"That's not friendship." Jairus shook his head, still frustrated at himself. "A friend doesn't turn his back when his brother is in trouble." He closed his eyes for a moment, and when he opened them he could feel the beginning of tears. "I learned that from Jesus."

"Real friends spend time together. Something Jesus taught me just last week."

Jairus smiled. "Maybe we can start again, you and I."

"Yes." Simon nodded. "I'd like that."

"I have to get back to my family. But I'm very concerned about Jesus. Before I go, there's something we need to do."

Simon seemed to understand exactly. They couldn't make the religious leaders listen. They couldn't stop the people of Jerusalem if—in the coming days—they turned on the Master. But there was something they could do to make a difference. And with that the two men bowed their heads.

And they prayed for their friend Jesus.

CHAPTER 4

# Mary Magdalene, the Demon-Possessed

### . . . And Jesus, the Friend Who Restores

*Never mind the seven demons* that had tormented her most of her life. All of the pain they had ever caused her paled in comparison to how Mary Magdalene felt right here. Right now. She kept up with the crowd, making her way toward the hill of Golgotha, her eyes on Jesus.

Her eyes on the cross.

Breathing was almost impossible. She gasped, trying to fill her lungs with even the slightest bit of air. But even then her heart broke inside her. She would never be the same after this. She might not survive it. Mary could do nothing but stay by His side. Her Jesus. Dust from the moving crowd kicked up and mixed with the tears on her face.

How could they do this to Him?

She studied His blood-covered, battered cheeks and forehead. The sharp crown of thorns they'd pressed into His skull dripped blood from a dozen places. But that was only the beginning of what they'd done to her Lord.

"Jesus!" she called out, but her voice died with the sounds of the crowd. "We're here! We won't leave You!"

Mary Magdalene reached back for the hand of the other Mary—the mother of Jesus. "We need to keep up."

"Yes." His mother looked weary. As if the pain of seeing Jesus suffer might actually kill her. She wiped the dust from her lips and looked at Jesus, then back at Mary Magdalene. "I'm trying."

Others were with them, including John—the youngest of the followers of Jesus. Most of His disciples were missing, though. Cowards. Scattered the moment Jesus was arrested. Only John had returned to be here with Jesus. At His most desperate hour.

The crowd shifted as it moved, and Mary caught a glimpse of Jesus's back. Whip marks lined it like so many ridges on a coin. His flesh hung in ribbons; blood and fluids oozed out.

And then there was the cross.

The soldiers had clearly made it of rough-hewn wood, because the splinters along its surface stuck out like very visible spikes. The Roman soldiers obviously didn't care.

This was always the way with crucifixions. But typically someone else carried the prisoner's cross.

Not so with Jesus.

The cross had to weigh at least twice as much as a grown man. It was three times as tall as Jesus and twice as wide. Yet the soldiers made Jesus carry it on His back. On His raw, ripped-apart flesh. Mary's heart felt like it might stop beating. Watching Jesus suffer was more than she could bear. *God, why are You allowing this? He's Your Son!*

Her silent prayer garnered no answer, no hopeful response.

Mary hurried to keep up. Jesus had been the greatest friend she'd ever known. The one who had seen past the demons, to her heart, buried deep inside. When no one else cared. From the beginning Jesus had never seen her as the afflicted woman. He hadn't seen her for what she was—but rather for what she could be.

She would be devoted to Him forever—no matter what happened in the next few hours. He had stepped into her poisonous madness when she only wanted to die. He had forgiven her and healed her. He had set her free. She would be indebted to Him as long as she drew breath.

Mary looked ahead. They were getting closer to Golgotha. Closer to the hill where the crucifixion would take place. Not just Jesus, but the two prisoners trudging along behind Him. They were villains, robbers. Criminals. But Jesus had done nothing wrong.

He had healed the sick, given sight to the blind and

raised the dead to life. He was the Messiah. God with them. And because of His simple, honest claim, the religious leaders were going to crucify Him.

Mary thought back to the beginning of this awful day, to the hour when Jesus was arrested. She was there again, waiting at the edge of the Garden of Gethsemane, looking for Jesus. She expected to see Him and His closest followers exiting the garden, ready for whatever was next.

Instead a band of soldiers had stormed the gate and gone after Jesus. Mary scrambled to follow them, but she could do nothing to stop Him from being arrested.

Only then did she see who was behind the awful betrayal.

Judas. One of the twelve.

The twelve disciples were first in line after Jesus, wherever the group had traveled for the last few years. Mary Magdalene and Mary, His mother, and the other women stayed near the back of the group. They prayed and bought food with their own funds and made sure Jesus and His followers had a place to stay.

But the twelve came first.

And here one of them had betrayed Jesus. The very memory of Judas kissing Jesus on the cheek—as a way of identifying Him to the soldiers—made Mary Magdalene sick. But that had been only the beginning.

Mary and the other women followed Jesus to His trial. She knew it was a mockery of justice. A trial in the dead of night with no proper witnesses. In fact, talk in the courtyard was that the few witnesses who stepped forward were liars. Lying on purpose to see Jesus put to death. She and the women were there in the shadows in Pilate's Hall, where the religious leaders—the Sadducees and Pharisees—clamored for Jesus's death. Once when she cried out for Jesus a soldier jolted her with the blunt end of his sword.

"Say another word, and you'll be thrown in prison."

And so Mary Magdalene stayed quiet. She needed to be near Jesus, needed to serve Him however she could. Prison would allow her no way to help her Master, her friend.

Then, Mary listened while Pontius Pilate asked the people who they wanted freed. Jesus or Barabbas. And she was there to see the religious leaders infiltrate the crowd of people outside the courts, rallying them to free Barabbas. Urging them to crucify Jesus.

She would forever hear their barbaric shouts, "Away with Him! Crucify Him!" The words ripped into her heart. She couldn't bear to hear them talk that way about her friend. The One who had given her life.

Mary had watched as Pilate made his decision. Jesus would be crucified. And she watched as the man washed his hands of his decision. Mary had felt both anger and pity for Pilate. He might order the crucifixion of Jesus with clean hands. But the man's soul would never be clean of the deed he'd committed.

And now she was here, taking this terrible walk alongside Jesus. A walk in which she could do nothing but watch. She pressed her way through the crowd, stopping

occasionally for Mary, His mother, to catch up. A man jos-
tling along beside her brushed against her arm.

"Well, hello, beautiful woman! You're too pretty to be
one of His followers." He glanced at her, his eyes dark
with trouble.

"He is my Master. My Savior." Mary shouted the
words as she jerked away from the man. The push of the
crowd placed other people in the space between him and
her. The man stared at her over the heads of several people, but then he moved on.

Mary wondered what the man would've said if he
could've seen how she'd looked before Jesus. Most days
she tried not to remember that time of her life. Back
when she was possessed of seven demons. But here—
with her eyes on her dying Lord—it seemed only fitting
that she allow herself to remember.

*Most people in Magdala* knew Mary's story. Some had become followers of Jesus as a result. But here in Jerusalem,
Mary was seen as merely another follower.

Nothing could've been further from the truth.

Magdala was a prosperous town, and Mary's family
had been wealthier than most. The trouble began some-
time after her twenty-first birthday. One day she was well,
tending to her family's business, friends with the right
people, owner of a beautiful home and the finest clothing.
In addition, she was very beautiful. She had long dark hair
and a smooth complexion.

She was pledged to be married to the richest, most handsome man in the city. It was Mary's third betrothal. The first two men had died of illness and now the townspeople saw her as getting on in her years. Back then Mary didn't care. She wasn't in a hurry. Men were good to her. She knew how to use her body to keep their attention. Her mother reminded her that she needed to watch her behavior. Jewish law had strict rules about the purity of women.

Mary didn't care about that, either. She wasn't even sure she believed in God. Anyway, one day soon she would marry her fiancé and settle down. Until then, life was great. The parties and jewelry, the men she saw on the side, her expensive home—all of it was hers for the taking.

It had been her birthday. She could still remember going to sleep that night, the night everything changed. A thought had crossed Mary's mind before she closed her eyes. Life simply could not get better. Mary Magdalene had it all. But overnight something happened, something wicked and evil. Because in the morning when she woke up she could hear screeching and wailing. Bloodcurdling screams that ran through the recesses of her mind.

In a rush, Mary tore out of bed and ran for her mother. "Can you hear it? The screeching and crying? The screaming?" Her shout filled the room. "Who is it? What's happening?" She felt like a crazy person. "Please tell me you can hear it!" She put her hands over her ears. "Mother, it's deafening!"

Her mother's expression was all the answer she needed. The woman's eyes grew wide with alarm and she led Mary back to her bedroom. Together they sat at the edge of her bed. "Mary, you must be dreaming. Darling, no one is making a sound. You're at home."

Mary shook her head, frantic for her mother to understand. "I know I'm home. But the noise . . . Mother, listen!"

The screeching was like the awful cry of a prehistoric animal. The wailing, as if every person and every moment of grief in all the world were combined in the voices. And the screaming . . . the screaming was the worst of all. As if hordes of people were being dragged through the gates of Hades.

Then the sounds grew louder. "Mother!" Mary screamed. She pressed her hands against her ears and shook her head. Harder and harder still. "Make it stop! Please!"

Her mother's face drained of color. "Stay here. I'll get help."

Mary had no idea how long her mother was gone, but it felt like days. Alone in her room the sounds consumed her, filling her heart and soul until she couldn't stand them another moment. She curled up in her bed, her knees tucked to her chest. Then she began pulling at her hair and clawing at her face, her ears, her arms.

By the time her mother returned with a doctor, Mary held tight to fistfuls of her beautiful locks. The hair was wet with Mary's blood.

Her mother fell to her knees at Mary's feet and cried

out loud. "Mary! My daughter, what have you done?" She grabbed at Mary's feet and then she went limp, passed out on the floor.

The doctor looked panicked now, too. He helped Mary's mother first, using sniffing oils to help rouse her and moving her to the other room. For a brief moment, the terrible sounds in Mary's head grew quiet. The doctor returned to her, his eyes wide with horror.

"Doctor?" Mary stood, breathless from the ordeal of the past hour. "What is it?"

He took a step back. "Your . . . your face. Your arms."

Mary looked down. There were claw marks running the length of her arms. As if she'd been attacked by a frenzied animal. Only no one but Mary had been in the room the entire time her mother was gone. "What . . . what happened?" Mary's scream was loud and shrill. "Doctor, help me!"

She felt her face next and the damage there was much the same. Deep claw marks trailed down her forehead and cheeks. Even her nose was bleeding. She began to shake. "Doctor, help!"

Instead the man shook his head, still staring at her. Then, as if he were running from a monster, he turned and fled the room. As he left, Mary heard a sound at the door. The sound of a key turning.

"Doctor!" She ran to the door, but it wouldn't budge. He had locked her inside. Without food or water or bandages for her wounds. Without any hope whatsoever, she was trapped in her bedroom. And as soon as she realized what had happened to her, how even the doctor didn't want to be near her, the sounds returned.

This time louder still.

Mary covered her ears and then, like before, she began pulling at her hair, scratching at her face. "Stop! Someone make it stop!"

But the sounds only grew worse and an ocean of terror flooded her veins. Mary had never known anything like the desperate feeling that overcame her in that moment. Yes, she had been frightened before. Years ago when her father grew sick and died, Mary had feared for their ability to survive without him.

But this . . . this feeling of utter, horrifying terror was something altogether different. The sounds consumed her. Mary gasped for breath, grabbing at her throat. She slithered to the ground, her heart pounding. Only with short, desperate gasps could she fill her lungs with any air at all. "M-M-Mother! H-h-help me!"

Something was trying to kill her. Something or someone. That's when she noticed terrible slimy, leathery beings coming at her, hissing at her, ready to kill her. Like bats, but they were the size of sheep and had sharp fangs. Mary swung at them again and again. But each time she only hit the edge of her bed or the floor or the wall. Finally she made it to her feet and dragged herself to the door.

For two minutes she pounded at it, screaming for the doctor or her mother. Anyone who might help her. Two whole minutes until her hands were bruised and swollen.

The scary, dark beings were closing in on her. She could smell them. A pungent sulfur. Mary threw herself to the ground and began flailing her arms and legs until finally the beings retreated. But they were waiting for her. There on either side of her bedroom door.

The screeching grew louder and time stood still.

Mary had no idea how long she sat there, tormented on the floor of her bedroom. At some point she must've fallen asleep because when she woke up again she was no longer in her safe, beautiful home. No longer just down the hall from her mother.

She was alone, in a strange room. In a home she didn't know.

A doctor came in and explained the situation to her. "Mary, your mother arranged for you to be sent here with me. She's paying me to . . . take care of you." He put his hand on her shoulder. "You are possessed by evil spirits." He looked defeated. "Your case . . . it's the worst I've seen."

"What?" Mary put her hands over her ears. The people in her head were screaming again. She clenched her fists so she wouldn't claw her face. "Why . . . why has this happened?"

The doctor shook his head. "I don't know. The demons hate people. They seek to kill and destroy. That much I've seen personally." He hesitated, as if he didn't want to tell her this next part. "Your mother brought you here. Until . . ."

"Until?" Terror took her breath. She couldn't fill her lungs.

"Until the situation changes."

She began to shake, her feet tapping on the floor, her teeth chattering. "I . . . haven't . . . done anything . . . to deserve this."

Mary could not believe what had happened to her. One day she was the most beautiful, most privileged young woman in town. And now . . . now she was demon-possessed? The situation was more than she could bear. And the more she realized how grave her new reality was, the louder the screeching and wailing and screaming grew.

Finally she could bear it no longer. In a vicious thrust of her hands, she dug her fingernails into her face and arms. "Make . . . it . . . stop!"

Then the doctor took Mary's arms and bound them together behind her back. "I'm sorry, Mary. This is for your own good."

"You'll pay for this!" Mary heard her voice, heard the way she hissed the words. But she had never intended to say them. Nausea pushed through her insides. Who was speaking for her?

Demons?

Mary squeezed her eyes shut and tried to break free from the cloth ties around her wrists. She tried with all her might, but she failed. If this was demon possession, she would rather die.

*Throw yourself in the fire, Mary,* a voice screamed at her. *Go into the back courtyard and throw yourself into the fire!*

It was the demons. It had to be. She had never heard a more acidic, angry voice in all her life. She began to kick and thrash about. Even with her arms tied behind her back, she managed to throw herself to the floor.

As she did, her skin began to itch. Not an ordinary itch, but the kind that ran from the depths of her soul to the surface of her skin. An itch no scratching could touch—and with her hands tied, Mary couldn't scratch at all.

The rest of the afternoon Mary thrashed about. Sometimes the voices grew dim, but when they did, the dark figures closed in on her. With her hands tied, she could do nothing about them. Nothing but scream. And so she screamed and screamed and hissed at the beings until finally she had no voice left.

Then with sides heaving from the exertion, Mary fell asleep.

The next morning she was wakened by deafening screeches, terrible screams, and something worse than before: a terrible evil laughter and the horror of her new existence.

The doctor was clearly right. Mary was possessed by demons. Not one. She was possessed by seven. She could count the different voices. Officially she was a demoniac—a person fully and completely possessed by evil. Mary had just one question for the man. "Please . . . can you kill me? I don't want to live like this!"

But the man only shook his head. "It is not right to take a life, Mary. Jewish law prohibits that."

Jewish law.

"What . . . good does . . . the law do me now?" She hissed at the doctor and a different voice came from her. "Get back, heathen! Stay away from me!"

The doctor took a few steps back. Concern was heavy in his expression. "Mary . . . there is One I believe might help you. I have sent for Him."

"You're a liar! You belong in the miry pit with the other demons!" Again the voice was not her own. Then her normal voice returned. "Please! Set me free, Doctor! Take off the cloths around my hands and feet!" She gasped for breath. "Who . . . who can help me?"

"Jesus."

"No! Lies! Shut up and leave me alone!" This time the voice was that of a man. Mary thrashed from one side of the table to the other. Then gradually she grew still. At the sound of the name of Jesus, the voices in her head grew quiet. The quietest they'd been since the first day.

Mary glanced around the room looking for the evil shadowy figures. But the only one standing before her was the doctor. Her body ached from exhaustion, but she had to understand exactly what the man had told her. "Jesus?" She grabbed three quick breaths. "His name . . . is Jesus?"

This was the best Mary had felt since that first morning. Almost as if she were in her right mind. "Can you . . . get Him for me? I'll . . . pay anything." Her mind raced. "And tell my mother to come. Where is she?"

The doctor looked even more uneasy. "Your mother . . . she grew sick after you came here." He looked down at his feet and after half a minute he found her eyes again. "She's dead, Mary. I'm sorry."

Mary began to shake again; she rolled onto her side and threw up. Again and again and again. Until she was heaving up nothing but air. As if her body was desperate to take her back to the night before all this happened.

"Please . . . get Jesus for me!" She could barely speak the words. But again, at the name of Jesus she felt a settling deep inside her. A sensation she couldn't explain.

This time the doctor's eyes softened. As if he held out just the smallest bit of hope. "I have to be honest with you. It could be months before Jesus passes this way. Years. Maybe not at all." He folded his arms. "But if He comes to our town . . . I will bring Him here. You have my word."

Fear pressed in around her heart and soul, and from the edges of the room the leathery bat-like beings began closing in on her again. A screech ran through her mind and then the cacophony of screeching and screaming and wailing. And deep inside her brain someone began to laugh at her.

"It's a lie! Get out of here!" The voice was not her own, but Mary could do nothing about the fact. The doctor left the room and when he returned he had a rag in his hands.

"Don't move, Mary. This is for your own good."

She began thrashing about the bed, frantic to set her hands and feet free. But before she could do anything to stop him, the doctor placed the rag against her nose and mouth. A strong smell filled her senses and Mary felt her body relax. She suddenly lay very still. And though the horrific noise continued in her mind, her body could no longer keep up the fight.

She couldn't battle the demons another day. Even worse, Mary no longer cared. It was too late. The demons owned her now.

And Jesus was nowhere to be found.

*Death wouldn't come. No* matter how many times she asked or how hard she tried to bring it on herself. The demons had found a home in her and they weren't about to leave. Mary had been fighting them, living with hands and feet bound most of the time, for nearly two years when finally . . . finally, word came.

Jesus, the Teacher, was coming to Magdala.

Mary's doctor was the first to tell her. He woke her up that morning and sat at a distance. "Mary . . . Jesus is coming. I've sent word, asking Him to stop by our home."

Beautiful calm filled Mary—body, heart, mind and soul. She didn't dare move, didn't do anything but stare at the doctor. "Will He come here?"

The doctor looked uncertain. "Reports are widespread. He is the Healer. Every town He comes to Jesus makes the lame walk, He cures diseases and casts out demons. Some say He even touches the lepers." The doctor hesitated. "If that's true, then maybe He will come here."

Mary moved just a little. Her hands and feet were tied to the bed from the night before. "Please . . . unbind me. The voices are quiet for now."

He looked reluctant. Everyone was afraid of Mary. The housekeepers and gardener. No one had ever seen anyone as afflicted as Mary Magdalene. Slowly, tentatively, he stood and approached her. "What about the figures? Do you see the figures, Mary?"

"No." She sounded well. In her right mind.

The doctor untied her hands and feet. He moved to the door and talked to her from there. "Have you prayed to the Father about your condition?"

Mary didn't speak.

"Do you want Jesus to come to you?" The doctor looked convinced. "If He is the Healer, Mary, maybe He will change your life if you ask Him."

Mary looked away. "Thank you, Doctor." Her lips were swollen, cracked and dry. There was a taste of blood in her mouth—maybe because she was dehydrated. Or maybe she'd bit her lips during the night. A sigh filtered from her broken heart. Could Jesus really change things for her at this point? Mary didn't dare hope.

The doctor left and Mary heard the sound of the key locking the door. Like that, she was alone again. She stared at the wall. *Jesus.* If He was the Healer, then maybe the doctor was right. Maybe He was her only hope.

But what if Jesus was just another fraud? Like so many other healers?

Suddenly she was seized by the familiar, fierce, itch-ing sensation. It moved from her feet to her head, to her middle and then to someplace deep inside. Mary followed it, scratching intensely at herself. But when the terrible feeling moved inward, she could do nothing to relieve it.

The screaming voices started and then the screeching. The laughing. The guttural wailing. Mary's mind shook from the noise until it was impossible to think or move or hope for anything. Impossible to think about Jesus coming to see her.

Even if she wanted to.

*They had reached Golgotha.*

The memory of Mary's past faded in a hurry and she stared at the scene before her. All of her attention was needed here, in the present. The soldiers had thrown the cross to the ground and now . . . Mary swept her thick, beautiful hair back and covered her eyes.

"No . . . God, don't let them do this to Jesus!" She began to weep into her hands. "Where are You, Father?"

On her other side, Mary, His mother, was weeping also. The disciple John stood at her side, comforting her. Mary uncovered her eyes and looked at Jesus. She couldn't hide her eyes. If there was a single moment when she might say something or do something to help Him, Mary wanted to be ready.

The way Jesus had been ready to help her back in Magdala.

A Roman soldier placed a spike over one of Jesus's

wrists. Then with a single powerful motion he raised his hammer and brought it down squarely on the enormous nail, driving it through Jesus's flesh.

"No!" Mary Magdalene screamed out. "Don't do this!"

This time a guard was standing closer. He picked up a handful of dirt and threw it in Mary's face. "You're next if you're not careful."

Mary's tears came harder, sobs took over her ability to breathe or speak or move. It was really happening. Jesus was being crucified before her eyes and there was nothing she could do about it. She might as well have been bound to the bed again for all the good she could do for Him.

But just then . . . just when she felt the depth of anger at her own ineptitude, Mary remembered something Jesus had said. One night when His followers were gathered around the fire, done for the day, He had been talking to them about love, about remaining in His love and keeping His commands. He added that His joy would be complete as they loved one another and as they remained in the Father's love.

He had paused then, and added another point. Something Mary remembered now as clearly as if Jesus had just spoken the words. Jesus had looked at each of them, His kindness and concern for them clearly evident. "Greater love has no one than this . . ." His words felt weighted with a desperate sense of purpose. "To lay down one's life for one's friends."

Now she understood. Jesus had told them that the greatest love a person could show his friends was to die for them. There were other statements Jesus had made in the weeks leading up to this awful day. Several times He had talked about how He would be handed over to the high priests and killed.

The guards were hammering a spike through Jesus's other wrist, and Mary gasped, bringing her hands to her face so she wouldn't have to look. But even as she did, peace settled in her battered spirit. It washed over her and suddenly she felt like she was standing on holy ground.

She hated this, hated seeing anyone speak sharply to Jesus, let alone torture Him. But everything Jesus ever said had been true. Every word. Every promise. If He needed to die here, then it would be for one reason.

So that all of them might live.

There was a plan at work, Mary could feel it to her core. Just like there had been a plan when Jesus made His way to the house where she lived back in Magdala. Mary closed her eyes. So she wouldn't have to see them drive the nail through Jesus's ankles. But also because she was back there again, tied to her bed.

Wondering whether Jesus would really come to her or not.

*She was locked in* the room, tied to the bed when there was a sound at the door. The strangest thing, the detail Mary would always remember, was the fact that the person on the other side used no key in the door. She had heard no sound of the lock turning. The door simply opened, and standing there was Jesus.

Mary didn't need to ask His name. She knew as surely as her next breath. She opened her mouth to say *Jesus*, to speak the name that had brought her the only comfort she'd known since the demons moved in. But instead her voice became that of someone else. "Don't torture us!"

Fear clamped its grip on Mary's neck, on her heart. She gasped for breath, desperately trying to grab at her throat. But no matter how afraid Mary felt, Jesus remained the picture of calm. His eyes spoke to her before He said a word.

He came closer, His presence both calm and authoritative. The closer Jesus drew to the edge of her bed, the more she could feel the demons respond. As badly as they tormented her, as terrified as they made her, they were far more afraid of Jesus.

Whatever Jesus said next, Mary wasn't sure. The screeching and wailing in her head was worse than ever before. She was bound hand and foot so she couldn't scratch at herself or rail at the walls. The screams were coming from her own mouth now, mixing with the ones in her head.

Jesus held out His arm and with a touch she would remember forever, He pressed His hand against her forehead. Whatever He said, whatever powerful life-giving words came from His mouth, Mary couldn't hear them. She still had no idea what He'd done with the demons, where He'd sent them.

She only knew that with a violent rush of motion and noise and pain, suddenly everything was still. Still in a way Mary hadn't known since that terrible morning after her birthday. Her chest heaved from the exertion, but other than the sound of her breathing the horrible noises were gone.

The doctor was at the door, his face stricken. "Jesus . . . Master." The man was more learned than anyone Mary had ever met. People came to him from many regions away for his ability to help the sick. But in that moment—in the presence of Jesus—the doctor dropped to his knees, his face to the floor. "Glory be to God."

Jesus touched the man's shoulder. "Release her."

In a scramble, the doctor stood and untied Mary's hands and then her feet.

Tears streamed from Mary's eyes. The demons were gone. Banished. This was what freedom felt like. Mary had almost forgotten. She covered her face, overwhelmed in the powerful presence of the Savior. When she lowered her arms, Jesus was still standing there, watching her. She sat up and turned to place her feet on the floor. "Thank You." She stared at Him, and suddenly she knew how she would spend the rest of her life. "Master, wherever You go, I will go."

"Yes, Mary. Follow Me." Jesus's eyes pierced hers. As if He had known her since before she was born. He didn't have to tell her to stop sinning, to believe in Him and to change her arrogant, impure ways. He didn't need to spell out the fact that she'd been promiscuous and unfaithful. Those things were evident in His eyes.

Instead He left the room and returned to His place outside with His disciples. Mary gathered her things in a matter of minutes. People from nearby had come close to the house. They wanted details. How had it happened? What had she said? Where was she going? Mary said just one thing as she left the house for good.

"Jesus set me free."

There was nothing more to say. On her way out of Magdala, Mary gathered the money that was rightfully hers. Money from her family's business. Before Jesus had set her free, before the demons, Mary had enjoyed having money. It allowed her to do what she wanted, dress and buy and go where she pleased. Now—like everything else about her life—the money didn't belong to her.

It belonged to Jesus.

*Mary kept her word.* She followed Jesus wherever He went, staying with Jesus's mother and a group of women with similar experiences. Women who were set free by the touch of the Master's hand. Together Mary and the other women provided support for Jesus and His followers.

The joy of giving never grew old for Mary. Neither did the thrill of watching Jesus do for other people what He had done for her. Not only did Jesus set people free from demon possession—He would give sight to the blind, legs to the lame, and life to the dead.

Mary's favorite moments were right after Jesus healed someone. The look of complete and utter peace, followed by a look of shock and freedom. Freedom most of all. Two of the healings of Jesus stayed with Mary more than the others. Maybe because she could relate to them personally.

The first was a man like Mary, a man possessed by demons. The man roamed a cluster of caves, naked and lashing out. Mary had wept, staring at the way the horror consumed him, watching the way he was instantly in his right mind with just a word from Jesus.

Mary knew what that sort of demon possession felt like. But that afternoon she had a clearer picture of what it *looked* like.

Another moment Mary would always remember was the one in Bethany recently. Seeing the dead Lazarus walk from the tomb, the graveclothes hanging from his perfectly healed body. Death would never have the last word with Jesus. No matter how much His people suffered, no matter how illness or accident took the lives of His followers— death couldn't stand up to Jesus.

So when He spoke to His followers about being killed and raised on the third day, Mary figured she must not have understood. Surely He must've been talking about something else. Because where there was Jesus, there was life. Every possible kind of life. Until now. Mary hadn't thought anyone could ever harm the Master, the Savior.

But she had been wrong.

\*  \*  \*

*The cross was standing* upright now. Death wasn't far off.

The Master who had given so many the ability to breathe was struggling for every breath. The one who had made the paralyzed walk could not take a step. Mary could only look for a few seconds at a time before turning away. *God, rescue Him . . . set Him free! Show Your power, please!*

No matter how desperately Mary begged, her prayers had gone unanswered. Jesus was still up on the cross. Still dying. She was comforted only by His recent statements about how the greatest gift of friendship was to lay down one's life for another.

Remembering His words brought purpose to the horror playing out before them. But they didn't make the ordeal bearable. Jesus called out several times as He gasped for air. The first time His statement was filled with the sort of mercy that would always set Jesus apart. With His eyes on heaven He cried, "Father, forgive them, for they know not what they do."

There were two thieves being crucified on either side of Jesus. One of them defended the Master to the other. Mary was touched deeply by what Jesus did next. Showing the same sort of indescribable grace He had long ago shown Mary, Jesus turned to the believing thief and— despite the effort each word cost Him—He spoke freedom over the man's final hours. "Today, you will be with Me in Paradise."

Next Jesus looked to His mother. Mary Magdalene had been very close friends with Jesus's mother throughout their time following Him. Now, Mary Magdalene was not surprised that in Jesus's final moments on earth He would take care of His mother. He simply looked at His loyal disciple John, and then at His mother. "Behold your son; behold your mother."

Immediately John took Jesus's mother into his arms, protecting her as Jesus had requested. The sight seemed to bring Jesus a deeper level of peace—even as His face was marked with agony.

His next cry brought tears to Mary Magdalene's eyes. "My God, My God, why have You forsaken Me?"

Mary Magdalene was crushed. Her dying Master felt forsaken? If she could've broken through the line of guards and taken Him down off the cross herself, she would have. Anything so her Jesus wouldn't feel alone. Not only was He suffering physical torture, but He felt emotionally abandoned as well. It was more than she could take. Mary wondered if the earth was about to break open and swallow all the people of Jerusalem. How dare these arrogant men kill the Master? How could they place the Son of God on a cross? Did they not fear mocking Him this way? Mary closed her eyes and remembered the many parables Jesus had spoken. Parables about the vineyard and the wedding banquet.

In each of them, the son was killed. And anyone, even beggars and strangers, was allowed to partake in the feast originally intended for invited guests only.

At the time, Mary and the other followers had not understood the meaning in the stories. But now . . . yes, now the meaning was perfectly clear. If they killed the Son of God, then God would take the Kingdom of heaven from His children and make it available to others. Gentiles, maybe. People from generations yet to come.

Those who would believe in Jesus.

The final words of the Teacher were cries that seemed to come from the place of His deepest suffering. He admitted His desperate thirst, and a little while later—when Mary knew she couldn't take standing here at the foot of the cross another moment—Jesus declared, "It is finished." He lifted His eyes to heaven once more and cried out. "Father, into Your hands I commit My Spirit."

And then He was gone. Mary could almost watch His Spirit leave His body. As it did, the earth began to shake until all of them were on their knees. Bedlam broke out across the land and the sun grew dim. In the darkness, Mary huddled with Jesus's mother and John and a few devoted followers. But even as they kept close together, Mary could see tombs breaking open and dead people being brought to life and walking around.

A guard shouted from a few feet away, "Surely, this was the Son of God."

Mary wanted to scream at all of them. Of course Jesus was the Son of God. They had mocked Him and given Him a false trial and then crucified Him like a common criminal. And now, Mary was certain, the people would pay the price. The religious leaders had done what they set out to do. Jesus was dead.

Mary's closest friend was gone.

When the earth stopped quaking, the guards took the body of Jesus down from the cross. All of it happened in a blur for Mary. She stood alongside the others, tenderly wiping the blood and dirt from Jesus's now cold skin. But it was like she was in some kind of trance. Like she might never feel whole or alive again.

Mary spoke quietly to the other women about the obvious—they needed a burial place for Jesus's body. Throughout His travels in the regions surrounding Jerusalem, the women had combined their money to help support Jesus and His disciples. But now their money was nearly gone. They certainly did not have enough to purchase a tomb.

In her sadness, Mary stepped aside. She lifted her hands slightly from her sides and stared at the dark sky. *God . . . if this is all part of Your plan, then show us. Give us a way to properly care for His body. We need Your help.*

At almost the same time, a wise member of the Sanhedrin—Joseph of Arimathea—approached them. "I've been waiting for the Kingdom of God," he told them. "Now that I have seen it, I will go to Pilate. I have a tomb you can use for Jesus."

Mary gasped softly as the man spoke. God had answered her prayer! He had heard her cry and somehow—in the midst of the most tragic moment imaginable—one thing was certain: God was still with them. Somehow He was still in control.

His death must indeed be part of some grander plan. After all, Jesus, Himself, had spoken about this moment while He was still alive. Hope burst in her heart anew. Jesus had never lied to them, never broken a promise. His warnings about His death had not been figurative, the way they had all assumed.

They had been literal.

Mary shared her thoughts with the others as they awaited news about the tomb. Mary the mother of Jesus agreed. Even in this nightmare, Jesus had a plan. Someone had brought oils and spices to prepare His body. Mary Magdalene worked alongside the other Mary. "We shouldn't be surprised, really." Mary Magdalene pressed the backs of her hands against her cheeks even as fresh tears filled her eyes.

"Jesus predicted this very thing." Mary, His mother, looked down at Jesus. "The prophets predicted it. Even before He was born."

After a while they grew quiet, tending to Jesus's body, wiping tears from their cheeks. Mary Magdalene couldn't bear to look at His closed eyes. The eyes that had shown love and acceptance to her when everyone else was afraid to be in the same room.

She just wished there might have been a different way.

A few minutes later Joseph returned with Pilate's permission. Jesus would be buried in his tomb outside the city. Mary reminded herself about the statements Jesus had made regarding His death. Suddenly a dawning happened in her heart. Jesus hadn't only talked about His death. He had said He would rise again on the third day.

But what did that mean? Would He rise here or in heaven?

As they carried His prepared body into the tomb, as the men worked together to seal it with the enormous rock, like all of His followers, Mary struggled to keep hope.

If Jesus were alive, He'd know what to do, how to calm the storm that threatened to drown them. Without Him, no one seemed to know what to say or do.

The followers found a place to gather, not far from the tomb, in an upper room. Eventually Mary and Jesus's mother and the other women were joined by the eleven remaining disciples. Women didn't often take the lead in conversations, but Mary Magdalene felt compelled.

"Remember what Jesus said? He would be handed over to be killed, but on the third day He would rise again?"

The men lifted their eyes to her and then each of them looked away. "Please, Mary. Do not tell us this was how the Master intended His life to end."

One of the disciples crossed his arms, clearly upset. "We heard word on our way here. Judas has killed himself. Clearly overcome by guilt for his betrayal." He glanced at Mary. "Does that sound like part of some divine plan?"

Mary moved to a far corner of the room and stared out the window. The men were right. The situation was dismal and growing darker with every hour. Normally where Jesus was involved life got better—not worse. Where He was involved, they were used to witnessing one miracle after another. Thousands of people sharing a few pieces of bread and fish, demon-possessed men and women healed with a single word.

Mary felt her fleeting hope fade. Now it seemed like God had lost and evil had won. Not that God could ever actually be defeated, but maybe He had simply given up on them. The people of Jerusalem had killed Jesus. Not only that, but one of His closest followers had betrayed Him, and most of His disciples had deserted Him in fear. Peter had denied Jesus publicly. God had a right to be done with them all. *Fine,* God might have thought. If the people wanted to desert and betray Jesus, if they wanted to kill God's Son, so be it. All of heaven would turn its back on mankind.

They didn't deserve Jesus.

Mary blinked a few times. And as she did she heard a single voice. The voice of Jesus. *Don't be afraid.* Those were His words time and again. *Don't be afraid.* He was the friend to the fearful, the One who set her free from her demonic storm, the One who touched the leper. If He were here He wouldn't have wanted them to be afraid, cowering in the upper room.

She breathed deep. Time would tell. Jesus had told them plainly that He would be killed and raised to life on the third day. All they could do now was wait it out, see if God had given up on them. Or if this was all part of a very great intentional plan.

The greatest plan of salvation the world had ever seen.

*   *   *

*The moment Mary opened* her eyes that Sunday morning, she shot straight out from under the covers. Like most mornings she remembered the days when she couldn't get out of bed if she wanted to—back when her hands and feet were bound. Freedom never got old, and always it reminded her that Jesus was the Master. The Messiah.

He had set her free.

But now, what about Himself? Her breathing came in a series of hurried gasps. She needed to get to the tomb, even if no one would go with her. In a rush she dressed herself and added an extra cloak. The air outside would be cold and damp. This week was chillier than usual.

Before leaving the building she nudged a few of the men. "Let's go to the tomb," she whispered. "It's the third day."

"Shhh." Thomas squinted at her. "It's early, Mary. Go back to sleep."

"No!" She raised her voice. "Jesus said He'd rise from the dead on the third day. This is the third day!"

"Mary." Thomas was more awake now. He sat up and looked straight at her. "Jesus is dead. He didn't mean to be killed that way. It happened." He hesitated, his discouragement heavy in his expression as he lay back down. "Go back to sleep."

For a long moment Mary only stared at Thomas and then at the others, several of whom had opened their eyes and were listening to the conversation. Did they really doubt the Master? They had seen more miracles firsthand than any of them could count or remember. Jesus had predicted His death. So why were they disheartened? The Master always did what He said. This was just one more example.

Did they really doubt Him? After the very great evidence of their own eyes?

Mary the mother of Jesus and Salome—the mother of James and John—rose and found their cloaks. "We'll go with you." Salome sounded hopeful. "Everything you're saying is true, Mary."

"Thank you." Mary pulled her cloak tighter and turned away from the disciples. Let them stay here. She and the other women would stand guard at the tomb whether Jesus came back to life or not.

The tomb was close by, and even in the pitch dark of the early morning, Mary and the other women arrived quickly. But what they found made them cry out in fear. The stone that had blocked the mouth of the tomb was rolled aside! Mary's heart raced within her. What had the Roman soldiers done now? Was it them or the religious leaders? They had already crucified Him. Couldn't they stop these incessant attacks?

Mary and the others turned and ran back to the upper room as quickly as their feet would carry them. She tripped twice, but scrambled back up and kept running. She burst through the door and went to Simon Peter first. "Peter!" She shook him awake.

Peter sat up. John, too, his eyes wide.

"What is it, Mary?" Peter searched her eyes. "What's happened?"

"They have taken the Lord out of the tomb, and I don't know where they've put Him."

"What?" Peter was on his feet immediately. He was one of the disciples there the night Jesus was arrested. He had denied Jesus, denied even knowing Him. But not now. Peter would do anything to make up for his terrible decision. Mary was convinced of that much.

The other disciples and followers rolled over, muttering about it being too early to be up. But Peter and John were already putting on their cloaks and sandals. As soon as they were dressed, they ran out the front door, and Mary stayed close behind.

"Wait!" Mary did her best to keep up with the two men, but they seemed to be racing each other to the tomb. John arrived first. He peered into the cave and looked at strips of linen lying on the ground. The same strips that had covered Jesus's body.

Peter raced right past John, straight into the tomb. He knelt down and looked closely. "These . . . are His graveclothes." Peter picked up the pieces. "Why would they be here unless . . . ?" He reached for a separate linen wrap, the one that had been used for Jesus's face. "If someone had stolen His body, they wouldn't have unwrapped Him."

"He's not dead." John still looked overwhelmed. "I believe in Him. That's all I know."

Peter looked at John and then Mary. "I believe, also."

He lowered his eyes, the shame from his betrayal still evident. "I do believe."

"We need to tell the others." John took a few steps toward the upper room. "Come on!"

Like that, the two friends took off running back to the house.

But Mary stayed at the tomb. The sun was coming up now, casting light through the trees on the place where the rock had been rolled away. Tears gathered in Mary's eyes. She wasn't as sure as Peter and John. Was He dead or alive? Did someone take His body? Now they would never know whether He'd come back to life or not. They could have taken Him anywhere.

Mary's tears came harder. The sobs shook her shoulders, making her feel hopeless. She would've walked all day if it meant finding His body, but she didn't know which way to turn or what to do. *Father, where is He? Where is my Master?*

As the silent plea filled her heart, she saw something move. Something in the tomb. Without making a sound she inched closer to the opening of the small cave. Her knees shook and her heart pounded. She peered inside and what she saw made her gasp out loud.

Two men dressed in white were seated—right where Jesus's body had been. One of them sat at the head of the rocky platform, and the other at the foot. Their eyes were bright, and their clothes even brighter. Mary didn't have to ask. She knew immediately that these were not men.

They were angels.

"Woman." One of them spoke first. "Why are you crying?"

Mary's tears still slid down her face. She wiped the back of her hand gently across her cheeks. "They have taken my Lord away." Small sobs washed over her. "I don't know where they have put Him."

The other angel spoke to her. "Don't be alarmed. You are looking for Jesus the Nazarene, who was crucified. He has risen! He is not here. See the place where they laid Him?" The angel motioned to the empty place on the stone platform. "But go tell His disciples—and Peter—that Jesus is going ahead of you to Galilee. You will see Him, just as He told you."

Mary started to move, but someone was standing behind her. She could feel his shadow upon her, so she turned and saw a man a few feet away. The gardener for the grounds, probably. Mary was flustered, trying to understand what had happened to Jesus and wanting to believe what the angels said was true.

He took a step closer. "Woman, why are you crying? Who is it you are looking for?"

Mary didn't take time to look at the man's face. She was too overcome by what had happened. With barely a glance at the gardener, she spoke. "Sir, if you have carried Him away, tell me where you have put Him, and I will get Him."

Silence followed. A holy silence that moved through the air around Mary like a physical presence.

"Mary."

Before she could draw another breath, Mary knew who was speaking to her. The man standing a few feet away was not the gardener at all.

He was Jesus!

She turned and cried out, "Teacher!" He was alive! He had risen just like He said He would! Death had not trapped Him after all! Of course it hadn't!

Mary reached for His hands, but Jesus stepped back. "Do not hold on to Me, for I have not yet ascended to the Father."

There were always things Mary did not understand about Jesus. The way He healed people, His way of multiplying bread and fish. This situation was another one of those. He hadn't ascended to His Father? Mary blinked a few times and nodded. "Yes, Master." Whatever His words meant, she didn't need to know.

Jesus was alive!

A smile came over Him. "Go to My brothers and tell them I said, 'I am ascending to My Father and your Father, to My God and your God.'"

Mary wasn't sure if He meant now or later today. But again she didn't need to know. "Yes, Teacher . . . I'll go now!"

She ran as fast as she could back to the disciples, and this time when she burst through the door she shouted the news. "I have seen the Lord!"

Then she told them everything that had just happened. This time everyone was awake and listening. More than that, they wanted to see for themselves. But when they ran back to the tomb, no one was there. Not the angels, and not Jesus.

It wasn't until later that night, when they were gathered in the upper room with the door locked, that suddenly Jesus was there, standing in their midst. Mary moved closer to Jesus's mother near the side of the room. They watched as one at a time the disciples realized what had happened. Several of them fell to their knees. Others came toward Him and stopped, their mouths open, shocked.

Jesus was the first to speak. He nodded at them. "Peace be with you." Then he held out His arms and showed them the holes in His hands. He even showed them the place in His side where the spear had sliced into Him in His final moments on the cross.

Quiet murmurs came from each of the disciples. "It's Him! It really is!"

From where she stood, Mary Magdalene smiled. She needed no proof. She had been the first to see Jesus, the first to know that He had risen from the dead. She had never deserted Him, never doubted Him. She was the first to see their risen Savior. Now she might've been the only one who wasn't truly surprised by His appearance.

Not that it mattered. Mary could only bask in the joy of His presence. Jesus was alive and He was here! The friend who had stood by her when death would've been a welcome release was whole again. Standing a few feet away. There would never be any greater friend than Jesus. He was the friend who hadn't run from her in fear, the friend who had helped her and healed her. And now Jesus had proved His friendship for all of them in the most beautiful way.

He had died for them, taking on death to fulfill the Scriptures. His presence here in the upper room was proof of that and proof of something more. Mary smiled as she watched Jesus talking with the disciples. Jesus hadn't only battled death for His friends.

He had defeated it.

CHAPTER 5

# Peter, the Betrayer

## ... And Jesus, the Friend Who Forgives

*Jesus was alive, that's all* Peter could think about. He had seen the Master twice now. But both times Jesus had appeared in a group setting—to all His disciples. There had been no time for Peter to pull Jesus aside and talk to Him one-on-one. Which really weighed on Peter. After all, things hadn't exactly ended well between him and Jesus. Those days when Jesus was in the tomb had been the worst of Peter's life.

Since that beautiful Sunday morning Peter had longed for a deeper moment with Jesus, a chance to clear the air. A way to express his remorse and recommit himself to the purpose of the Master. Jesus had told them they would be fishers of men. But what were they supposed to do? How should they begin?

Peter couldn't picture walking into Jerusalem, finding a corner in the Temple courts and just speaking out. He'd be arrested and put to death as soon as he mentioned the name of Jesus. Which was fine, actually. Peter was willing now. He really was. Jesus was the resurrected Lord. The Messiah. Savior. The one all of Israel was waiting for.

But Peter didn't want to make a move without knowing exactly how Jesus wanted him to proceed. And since Jesus hadn't been around in the last few days, Peter needed to get back to work. Make a little money. So as night fell Peter was doing the one thing he still knew how to do.

He was fishing.

The Sea of Galilee was calm that night. Sitting with him in the twenty-five-foot boat were Thomas, Nathanael, James, John and a few other disciples. They'd been fishing for three hours, but they hadn't caught a single fish. Not one.

Peter stared at the distant horizon. "I wish Jesus were here." He breathed deep, filling his lungs with the salty night air. "He could tell us what to do next."

"He must have a plan." Thomas stared at his hands. He rubbed his wrists. "I'll never doubt Him again."

"Yeah." Peter uttered a sad chuckle. "Me, either."

The boat danced lightly on the calm swells. They were all fishermen, but since meeting Jesus, Peter and the guys were different. They were still a rough-looking group.

Still strong and smelly, still the worst dressers around. But their words were different now. Kinder. More thoughtful. Same with their tones and actions.

It was easy to see the difference, especially out here on the Sea of Galilee. This was where it had all begun, here on the distant shore. Peter was nearly thirty now—and strong as ever. Strongest of the guys. He pulled his empty nets from the water, dragged them across the deck of the boat and buried them in the gentle swells on the other side.

He had first met Jesus after a dismal night of fishing, a moment like this. Every fish in the Sea of Galilee had eluded them. The water had been calm then, too. Peter stared toward the shore and he could see it all playing out again.

Crowds of people had followed Jesus to the shore, listening to Him teach. Peter had heard about Jesus from John the Baptist. If Peter hadn't been so busy trying to make a living, he might've been one of those gathered along the shore, pressing in around Jesus that morning. But he had to fish.

That morning, Peter had finally brought his boat in, defeated by the futility of his efforts. He was washing his nets when Jesus climbed into his boat—more to get away from the pressing crowds than anything. At least it had seemed that way.

"Put out a little from shore." Jesus nodded to the open sea.

Peter didn't ask, he just did what Jesus said.

From the beginning there was something different about Jesus, the way He spoke to people, the way He taught. That first day, Peter sat at the far end of his boat and listened to Jesus, studied Him. With water as a buffer between Him and the crowd, Jesus raised His voice only to be heard above the sea breeze.

He told them that they ought to treat others the way they wanted to be treated. And above all that they should love the Lord their God with all their hearts, minds and souls. People shifted in the sand, their expressions knotted in curiosity or wide open with acceptance. Some grumbled. Others nodded.

When Jesus finished speaking, He dismissed the crowd. Then He turned to Peter and pointed toward the open water. "Put out into the deep seas, and let down the nets for a catch."

Peter appreciated the efforts of the Teacher. But if anyone knew fishing, Peter did. Jesus was the son of a carpenter. What would He know about when to put the nets in or where? Still . . . something about Jesus captured Peter's attention. God seemed to be very much with Him.

So Peter took a step closer to Jesus, his tone polite. "Master, we've worked hard all night and haven't caught anything." He set the boat further out to sea. "But because You say so, I will let down the nets."

Jesus simply waited.

It didn't take long for Peter to reach deep water. He looked at Jesus for His approval. "Here?"

"Yes." Jesus grinned. "Let down the nets."

There were other fishermen aboard the boat, but Peter didn't need help. He could handle the empty nets. In a single motion Peter threw them over one side of the boat. He watched them hit the water and even before they sank a few feet, fish began flooding them. Jumping into the nets.

More fish than Peter had ever seen.

His fellow fishermen came quickly and helped heave the bursting nets onto the boat. Peter motioned for another boat to come up alongside them. In it were Peter's business partners—James and John—the sons of Zebedee. "Hurry!" he shouted at them. "There's more fish than we can take on!"

James and John did as Peter asked and over the next ten minutes so many fish flooded the decks of both boats that they began to sink. "Get to shore!" Peter waved his hands frantically at his friends. "Hurry!"

Terrified they would be swallowed up by the sea, Peter turned to Jesus. Suddenly he could see Jesus for who He was. This was no ordinary man, no talented teacher. This was the Messiah. The one John the Baptist had spoken about. Peter fell at Jesus's knees and hung his head. "Go away from me, Lord; I am a sinful man!"

It was true. If Jesus had known the things Peter did, the filthy way he spoke around the other fishermen, the women he kept company with . . . the Master never would've climbed into his boat in the first place. The fish had come from Jesus—clearly. Never mind the water spilling into the boats. They could solve that problem later. Jesus was here. Peter could no longer stand in His presence.

Besides, whatever was happening with the fish and the sinking boats, Jesus did not look afraid. He held His hand out toward Peter, and spoke in a voice filled with authority and kindness. "Don't be afraid: from now on you will fish for people."

Slowly, Peter rose to his feet. The boats still held an enormous amount of fish, but now they were no longer sinking. The words of Jesus ran through Peter again and again as they made their way to shore. *From now on you will fish for people.*

Peter had looked at James and John, also making their way to the shore. They had clearly heard Jesus's words, because the looks on their faces were much like how Peter felt. With a simple command from the Master the danger had passed. Instead they were left with two boats full of the largest catches anyone had ever seen. Ten fishermen combined had never brought in half this many fish.

But the fish no longer mattered. Only the obvious fact that Jesus was the provider. He could do all things. And so there had never been any discussion or debating about His declaration that from now on they would be fishers of men. Jesus, the Messiah, had called them. The old had gone, the new had come.

And so Peter and James and John simply pulled their boats up on shore, left everything and followed Him.

\* \* \*

*The memory faded as* the first light of day cast a pink hue across the sea, bringing an end to the fruitless night. Peter pulled his empty nets out of the water and heaved them over the other side of the boat. There was still time to catch something.

But the next hour netted not a single fish. This was a rare moment for fishermen on the Sea of Galilee. Almost as if God were giving them a sign. As if He didn't want them to go back to catching fish. But rather to spend their days fishing for people.

If only Peter knew how or what to do next. If only he'd made things right with Jesus.

The sun was appearing on the horizon, and with every minute the chances of getting a fish waned. Peter's fellow disciples were caught up in a conversation about Jesus—when they would see Him next, how He would impart instructions to them, how crazy Thomas was to ever doubt Him.

Peter tuned them out. They needed to get back to shore and find food for the others. Peter stood and squinted toward the shore. Something was moving. Or someone, perhaps. He shielded his eyes and cupped his hands around his mouth. "Who goes there?"

The other disciples turned and stared at the figure. "If it's a fisherman," Thomas stood, "where's his boat?"

As the boat reached shallow water, Peter could see it was a man dressed in a simple cloak. Clearly not the garb of a fisherman. "Hello, there!"

The man turned and faced them, his feet at the edge

of the water. "Friends, haven't you any fish?" The voice was familiar.

They were closer now, but Peter couldn't decide if he knew the man or not. "No," he shouted. "Nothing."

The man motioned to one side. "Throw your net on the right side of the boat and you will find some."

A damp chill ran down Peter's arms and legs. He'd heard this sort of instruction before. Without waiting another minute, Peter grabbed at the nets and hurled them off the right side of the boat. He looked overboard as a million fish made their way into the boat, rushing the net in a way Peter had seen only one other time.

John stood and stared at him. Clearly he was thinking the same thing. "Peter. It is the Lord!"

The moment Peter heard that, he grabbed his outer garment, wrapped it around himself, and jumped into the water. Forget riding in to shore. He didn't have time to wait for the boat. He needed to get to Jesus now—even if that meant swimming a hundred yards, fully dressed, through the cold morning water.

This time Peter wasn't going to miss his chance.

As he swam, despite the way his cloak dragged him down, he kept his eyes fixed on the Master. The moment reminded him of another much like it. A time when Peter had done the impossible.

So long as he kept his eyes on Jesus.

\*    \*    \*

*It had been one* of the most difficult days in the ministry of Jesus. They had received the most horrible news that morning, that Jesus's cousin, John the Baptist, had been beheaded by Herod's men. Peter could still remember feeling like the ground had turned molten beneath his feet.

The shock had taken a while to sink in.

John the Baptist was the Elijah of their day, the one to prepare the way for Jesus. How could he have been murdered? None of them knew what to say or how to comfort each other. While they were figuring it out, Jesus had climbed into a small boat by Himself and sailed to a private cove.

Even then the people came, bringing their sick and demon-possessed, their blind and lame. As Jesus returned from His private grieving and saw the crowds, He had compassion for them and spent the rest of the day healing them. But Peter had watched the Master closely that day. Jesus was suffering, Peter could tell. Maybe that's why no one thought about feeding the crowd until nightfall. At that point Peter and a few of the disciples went to Jesus.

"Master." Peter hated interrupting Him. Especially when inside, His heart must've been breaking. "This is a remote place, and it's already getting late." Peter looked at the men with him. They were doing Jesus a favor here, looking for a plan where there was none. They all hoped He'd listen to their advice. Peter cleared his throat. "Let's send the crowds away so they can go to the villages and buy themselves some food."

The love in the eyes of Jesus never dimmed, no matter the situation. Not even in that moment, when He had every reason to be frustrated. Every reason to send the people away. Instead He looked straight back at Peter and the others. "They do not need to go away. You give them something to eat."

The disciples looked to Peter—the way they often did. He tried again. "Master, we have here only five loaves of bread and two fish."

Jesus remained patient. "Bring them here to Me." Then He climbed a ways up the hill and announced that the people should have a seat on the grass. It took a while for the enormous crowd to be seated, but when they were, Jesus held the five loaves and two fish and looked up to heaven. "Thank You, Father, for this food. Thank You for providing for us always. Even when it seems there is not enough."

Peter wouldn't have believed what happened next, except that he'd seen it with his own eyes. Jesus broke chunks off the bread and passed the pieces to the disciples, and the disciples did the same thing, passing the bread to the people. There was nowhere near enough food, of course.

But because of Jesus, the food multiplied right before their eyes. They would break off a piece of bread and pass it to the next person, and at the same time another few pieces would appear in the basket. Same with the fish. Over and over and over again. When the meal was finished, after everyone had eaten their fill, the disciples picked up twelve basketfuls of leftover broken pieces.

With the heartbreaking news about John the Baptist and the needs of the crowd, the day had been long and full of challenges. Finally Jesus sent the people home. As they left, He turned to Peter and the others. "Get into the boat and go ahead of Me to the other side of the sea."

Peter didn't dare ask Jesus why He wasn't joining them. The Master still had not gotten the chance to truly grieve the loss of His cousin. Of course He needed time alone. The only slight concern that troubled Peter as he set out in the boat with the disciples that night was the weather.

Storms could come up quickly on the Sea of Galilee. Already the wind was whipping up whitecaps on the open water. Peter studied the distant sea. Left to his own decision on the matter, he would've stayed ashore. But Jesus knew what He was doing.

There was no reason to doubt Him.

The hours passed slowly, the boat buffeted by the increasing wind and waves. Then, shortly before dawn, they saw a figure walking toward them on the stormy sea. Walking right on top of the water!

"It's a ghost!" Thomas was the first to cry out. "God, save us! It's a ghost!"

Peter squinted at the figure, and just as he recognized the Man's face, Jesus spoke to them. His voice carried above the sound of the storm. "Take courage!" He cried out. "It is I! Don't be afraid!"

No matter how hard he had tried over the years, Peter had never quite learned to filter his words. His friends had told him that sometimes it was better to listen. Process. Consider. Jesus had told him that, too. But usually Peter simply blurted out whatever thought passed through his mind.

That night on the rough stormy Sea of Galilee was no exception.

Peter struggled to his feet and shouted, "Lord, if it's You, tell me to come to You on the water!"

Jesus was closer now, maybe twenty yards away. He held out His hands to Peter. "Come."

Again Peter didn't stop to consider the dangers or the outcome or even the laws of nature. Jesus had said to come, and so that's what Peter did. Immediately he stepped out of the boat and walked on the water toward Jesus. His feet connected with the top of the sea as if it were solid ground, and as long as his eyes were on Jesus, Peter was not in danger.

But then reality slapped him with a spray of water from the closest whitecap. He could still remember the thoughts that raced through his head in that wonderful, terrifying moment. What was he doing? He couldn't walk on water. This was the deepest part of the sea, after all. In the middle of a storm like this, if Peter sank, he'd drown almost instantly.

The wind whipped at his damp cloak and the cold water covered his feet. And so Peter lowered his eyes from Jesus to the waves, and as he did, he began to sink. His body gasped for air as his hand shot straight toward Jesus. "Lord, save me!"

As soon as Peter cried out for help, Jesus reached out His hand. He caught Peter and pulled him back to the surface of the water. The storm raged around them, but Peter could only hear the voice of Jesus. "You of little faith. Why did you doubt?" His eyes held a deep sense of love and concern. But at that point they also held sorrow. An undeniable sorrow. As if the lack of faith on the part of Peter was something that deeply grieved Him.

Jesus helped Peter to the boat, and as they climbed inside the wind died down. The water was calm. The other disciples huddled together, eyes wide, trembling. Matthew cried out as he fell to his knees. "Truly, You are the Son of God!"

Peter already knew that about Jesus. He sat huddled at one end of the boat looking out at the calm sea where he had minutes ago walked on water. He ran his fingers down the arms of his covering. Of course Jesus was the Son of God.

His cloak was still dry.

*Peter kept swimming, hurrying* to the shore as fast as he could. Even still, he reached ground about the same time as the boat. Jesus had a fire going and a quick glance told Peter that the Master was cooking fish and bread. Peter dragged himself onto the sand but before he could speak, Jesus pointed back to the boat.

"Bring some of the fish you have just caught."

"Yes, Lord." Peter ran back to the boat and dragged the net ashore. Later he would learn that they'd caught 153 fish in the few seconds after obeying Jesus. Peter couldn't believe the net hadn't torn. He brought back a basketful of fish to Jesus, where now the other disciples had gathered also.

Jesus smiled at Peter and the others. "Come and have breakfast."

The men exchanged a look, astonished that this was, indeed, Jesus. They all knew He was the Lord. And so they did as He asked and sat with Him around the fire, sharing a breakfast of fresh-cooked fish and hot bread.

They talked about life in the upper room, how no one really knew what to do next. And they admitted that, from what they'd heard, things were still chaotic in Jerusalem. People knew about the empty tomb, but the religious leaders had started a lie that Jesus's disciples had taken His body.

Jesus acknowledged that there would always be doubters.

Peter listened intently. Was Jesus referring to him? To the way Peter had done the unthinkable the night Jesus was arrested? Peter wasn't hungry. So while the others ate breakfast with Jesus, Peter stared into the fire and remembered another fire on a cold dark night, one where the people gathered around him were not his friends.

They were his enemies.

* * *

*Of course Peter's betrayal* that night hadn't actually started around the hot coals in the Temple courts. It had started long before. No disciple experienced the highs and lows that Peter did as they followed Jesus throughout the regions of Judea. Even his walking on water that night was both a high and a low. He was always jumping ahead or blurting out something he shouldn't have said.

Like the afternoon when they arrived at the region of Caesarea Philippi. They were gathered for lunch and the crowds had not yet caught up to them. In the quiet of the day, Jesus turned to the disciples. "Who do people say the Son of Man is?"

They agreed on their answer, but Thomas did the talking. "Some say John the Baptist; others say Elijah; and still others Jeremiah or one of the prophets."

Jesus nodded, pensive. "But what about you?" he asked. "Who do you say I am?"

Peter had been the first to stand. He held his fist in the air, adamant. "You are the Messiah, the Son of the Living God."

A smile filled Jesus's face. "Blessed are you, Simon, for this was not revealed to you by flesh and blood, but by My Father in heaven."

Nothing had ever made Peter feel so proud. He had pleased the Master. It was a beautiful memory he would carry with him always. He bowed slightly. "Thank You, Lord."

Jesus wasn't finished. He looked intently at Peter. "I tell you that you are Peter, and on this rock I will build My church, and the gates of Hades will not overcome it. I will give you the keys of the kingdom of heaven; whatever you bind on earth will be bound in heaven, and whatever you loose on earth will be loosed in heaven."

Peter couldn't believe it. The words of Jesus seemed like something from a dream. Peter was basically being singled out as the chief disciple, the one Jesus trusted the most. The Master's words were full of strength and power. It was more than he could've imagined. Peter felt the gazes of the other disciples. How did they feel? Peter had been given the keys to the kingdom of heaven. It was a heavy responsibility, one Peter didn't quite understand. Definitely one he didn't deserve.

But still Jesus had chosen him.

Then, just as quickly, Peter went from being the one honored by Jesus to the one disciplined. Jesus had begun explaining that He must go to Jerusalem and suffer many things at the hands of the elders, the high priests and the teachers of the law, and that He must be killed and on the third day be raised to life.

Clearly Jesus knew what was about to happen. But at the time Peter felt indignant at the possibility. Jesus, killed by the religious leaders? Finally one time Peter took Jesus aside and rebuked Him. "Never, Lord!" His tone was stern. "This shall never happen to You!" If Jesus wanted to build His church on Peter, then Peter figured he ought to speak up.

Jesus looked shocked at Peter's statement. "Get behind Me, Satan! You are a stumbling block to Me; you do not have in mind the concerns of God, but of humans."

Then Jesus looked at the other disciples. "Whoever wants to be My disciple must deny themselves and take up their cross and follow Me. For whoever wants to save their life will lose it, but whoever loses their life for Me will find it." He looked back at Peter. "What good is it for someone to gain the whole world, yet forfeit their soul?"

At the time, Peter was so confused. Hurt, even. He had only wanted the best for Jesus. He would've laid down his life if it meant saving Jesus from death at the hands of the religious leaders. If he hadn't felt so strongly, he wouldn't have rebuked Jesus.

But how quickly Peter had forgotten not only defending Jesus.

But even knowing Him at all.

*Thinking back now, Peter* knew what had gone wrong.

He had forgotten the point of his role as chief disciple. His days stopped being about Jesus and started being about himself. His opinions, his preferences. That had to be it. Since Jesus had given him the name Peter, since Jesus had called him the rock upon which He would build His church, Peter recognized the problem. He thought he had all the answers.

His attitude cropped up again at the last supper they had together. After eating with His friends, Jesus took a washbasin and a towel and began to wash their feet. But when He came to Peter, Peter shook his head. His feet were dirty, disgusting. Jesus was the Messiah, and Peter . . . well, Peter was a dirty fisherman. "Lord, are You going to wash my feet?"

Jesus's tone held a patience that knew no limits. "You do not realize now what I am doing, but later you will understand."

The thought outraged Peter. There was simply no way the Savior should even think of touching his dirty feet. "No!" Peter took a step back. "You shall never wash my feet."

This time Jesus hesitated, his gaze aimed straight at Peter's heart. "Unless I wash you, you have no part with Me."

An understanding had resonated with Peter. But it was the wrong understanding. He figured Jesus meant literally. Peter had looked at Jesus, confused and a little frustrated. "Okay, then, Lord, not just my feet but my hands and my head as well!"

Jesus took a deep breath. He explained that washing their feet was not about having a bath. Rather it was about taking the dirtiest part of a man and making that person whole. As only He could do. Then dinner grew more awkward. Jesus talked much about His death, comparing the bread and the cup to His own body and blood, which had to be shed for them.

At that, silence fell over the table. No one wanted to think about Jesus being killed, His blood being shed. Peter's only sense of peace that night came from the expression on Jesus's face. He hadn't looked afraid. Concerned, yes. But Peter had to believe there was a plan to everything happening.

They sang a hymn after dinner and they followed Jesus out to the Mount of Olives. Again they were quiet. Peter figured his fellow disciples were taking in everything Jesus had told them. Same way he was. Jesus sat on a rocky outcropping at the edge of the mountain, and the disciples did the same. A breeze filtered up from the valley, but otherwise there wasn't a sound. After a long silence, Jesus slowly looked each of them in the eyes, one at a time. Then He sat a little straighter. "You will all fall away."

Alarm coursed through Peter. He saw the same reaction on the faces of the others. They would never fall away. These were Jesus's closest friends. They had followed Him for years—no matter the circumstances. Some people had loved them along the journey, yes. But others had hated them. And still none of them had fallen away. Why would they fall now?

Peter raised his hand and tried to stop the Master from saying another word. "Master, I would never—"

"For it is written"—Jesus looked straight at Peter, silencing him—"'I will strike the shepherd and the sheep will be scattered.'"

His words felt ominous. They hung over the place where they met like so many storm clouds. Peter could feel his frustration growing, his indignation taking over his ability to listen.

Jesus continued. "But after I have risen, I will go ahead of you into Galilee."

Peter couldn't take another word of this. He loved Jesus too much not to speak up. Maybe the others would fall away, but not him. He glanced around the circle and his frustration doubled. No one looked ready to speak. Peter gritted his teeth. Was there not anyone in the group who heard what Jesus had said?

Outrage filled his heart. Someone had to defend the Master. "Lord." He stood and clenched his fists. He could feel the heat in his face. His knees trembled. "Even if all fall away, I will not."

Peter expected to see relief on the face of Jesus. At least someone had stood up for Him, at least one of them had refused the possibility of ever falling away from Jesus! Instead, the Master remained calm, unmoving, His eyes still on Peter. He didn't look grateful or relieved at all. In fact, looking back, Peter understood now the expression on His face. Jesus looked hurt, but patient—all at the same time.

"Peter, truly I tell you"—Jesus leaned His forearms on His knees, His gaze more intent than before—"today— yes, tonight—before the rooster crows twice you yourself will deny Me three times."

In all the years Peter had followed Jesus, he had never been more shocked, never more hurt. Peter was the one who knew the truth about Jesus first. When everyone else struggled to grasp that He was the Messiah, the Savior, Peter had known. Jesus had chosen him, after all, to be the rock upon which He would build His church. That had to count for something. Certainly Jesus must be feeling very low about the threats coming from the religious leaders if He really thought Peter would deny Him. Jesus couldn't actually believe Peter—the leader of the disciples—would turn his back on Him.

Peter paced a few steps one way and then another. How could Jesus not know him better? He would never deny Jesus! Outrage and deep pain grew within Peter until finally he turned to Jesus. Tears welled in his eyes and his entire body trembled. "Even if I have to die with You, I will never disown You!"

Now that Peter had broken the tension, now that someone had made a declaration in support of Jesus, the others did the same. In quiet, less emphatic voices, they nodded and talked among themselves. "Never. Not us! We won't fall away!"

Jesus didn't respond, didn't say anything to acknowledge Peter's promise or the promises of the others. Instead He led them to another place—Gethsemane. Then He took just three of them—Peter, James, and John—the friends first called, the ones who used to work together even before meeting Jesus.

The Master spoke intently to them. "My soul is overwhelmed with sorrow." Tears filled His eyes and His words were barely audible. "To the point of death."

Peter was ready to lay down his life, ready to throw himself in front of anyone who might hurt the Teacher. "Lord . . . what can we do? How can we help?"

"Stay here." Jesus looked like the weight of the world was on His shoulders. "Keep watch."

Peter wasn't sure what happened next. He sat down with James and John, the three of them leaning against different trees. Peter remembered lifting his eyes to the starry sky above and praying. He did pray. At least he started out that way. But he was also very tired. The events of the last few days weighed on all of them.

*Stay awake,* he told himself. Jesus had asked such a small thing. *Stay awake and pray and keep watch!*

But no matter how stern he'd been with himself as Jesus walked away, somehow Peter and the others fell asleep. The next thing Peter remembered, Jesus was tapping him on the shoulder. "Simon . . . are you asleep?"

Peter jolted awake, horrified as he looked into Jesus's eyes. The fact that Jesus had not called him Peter, but rather Simon—his old name—was intentional. Peter knew without asking. He felt sick to his stomach. He shook his head, desperately sorry. "Master, I . . ." There were no words he could say, no excuse he could make.

"Couldn't you keep watch for one hour?"

"I meant to . . . I mean, I tried to, but . . ." Again, Peter couldn't complete his statement. Every word sounded pathetic. "I'm sorry, Lord. I am."

Jesus leaned against the nearest tree. His eyes were red, as if He'd been crying. He looked at the distant sleeping valley for a long while and then at Peter. "Watch and pray so that you will not fall into temptation."

"That was my plan, but I—"

"Peter." Jesus stopped him. "The spirit is willing. But the flesh is weak."

The other two disciples were awake now, listening, their expressions also filled with sorrow. Jesus asked them again to keep watch, to pray. And again they all agreed. Then Jesus left them once more.

Peter had never been so angry with himself. How could he have let Jesus down? Earlier that day he had been certain he was the single disciple who would support Jesus the most. And now he couldn't even stay awake?

The reality was sickening.

*Things couldn't have gotten* worse—at least that's what Peter had thought. He had his head against the tree a second time, and began to pray. But very quickly he felt his eyes grow heavy. *Stay awake! This is for Jesus!* He shook his head a few times and slapped his cheeks. Why was he so tired?

Again Peter could remember nothing else. Like before, he felt a touch on his arm. He woke with a start and stared— again—straight into the eyes of Jesus. "My Lord . . ."

This time Jesus said nothing. Not to Peter or James or John. He merely looked at them and then at the ground. He had never looked worse—His face tight with sorrow, His eyes red from crying, His robes dusty. Peter opened his mouth to speak, to explain himself. But no words would come.

His actions had said all there was to say.

When Jesus left them again, Peter sat up straighter. It would not happen now—not a third time. If Jesus wanted him to stay awake, to keep his eyes open and pray, then Peter would obey. No matter what. No amount of sleep was more important than doing the work of the Savior. Surely he could trade his own comfort for the chance to honor Jesus.

But even then, Peter fell asleep. James and John, too. All of them. The fishermen who had conquered storms and windy gales and earned a reputation for being the toughest in all of Galilee could not do what Jesus asked. They couldn't stay awake—not for a single hour.

This time when Jesus returned, His face was marked by streaks of blood mixed with dirt. He looked terrified and determined, hopeless and resolute. He sighed as He searched their tired faces. "Are you still sleeping and resting?" A flash of frustration crossed His eyes. "Enough! The hour has come. Look, the Son of Man is delivered into the hands of sinners."

Peter had blinked a few times. What was Jesus talking about? They were alone here, just the four of them. Certainly He couldn't be talking about Peter, James, and John. They were tired, but that didn't make them sinners, right? Peter was still trying to decipher whatever Jesus meant when He began to walk away. He looked back over His shoulder at them, more urgent than before. "Rise! Let us go!" He faced forward. "Here comes My betrayer!"

Peter had never been more scared in all his life. He scrambled to his feet and motioned for the others to do the same. Dusting off their garments, they followed Jesus down the path and almost immediately a large crowd of people came into view.

"What?" Peter gasped. Leading the crowd was Judas. Their own Judas. One of the twelve disciples. And suddenly Peter remembered Jesus saying that one of them would betray Him. Peter shook his head, furious at Judas. "No!" he shouted. "You can't do this!"

His words were lost in the noise and commotion of the crowd. Peter could make out their faces now. The crowd consisted of some of the same people who had thrown down their robes and palm branches and welcomed Jesus into Jerusalem just a week ago.

Now they were armed with swords and clubs, ready to kill the Master.

Judas walked straight up to Jesus, and for a single moment a hush fell over the angry mob. No one said a word. Then Judas smiled at Jesus. "Rabbi!" He leaned near and kissed Jesus on the cheek.

"Friend." Jesus paused. He put His hand on Judas's shoulder. "Do what you have come for."

Peter felt himself relax. Jesus had called Judas friend. Everything was going to be okay. Clearly this wasn't how it looked. Judas must've been leading the crowd somewhere else, to find the religious leaders who were spreading lies against Jesus. Yes, maybe that was it.

But as soon as Judas stepped back, the mob rushed in and seized Jesus. An official near the front of the crowd grabbed Jesus's arms. "You're under arrest!"

What was happening? Judas had betrayed Jesus with a kiss? Even while Jesus called him friend? Peter wasn't having it. He drew his sword from his robe and held it high over his head. They couldn't do this . . . they couldn't arrest Jesus! He rushed forward. "Leave Jesus alone!"

The servant of the high priest stepped up, blocking Peter from reaching the Master. "Stop!" He raised his club toward Peter.

"No!" Peter ran at the man and brought his sword down hard. In the process, he cut off the man's ear.

The servant of the high priest shouted in pain. Blood gushed from his head and he stared at his ear, now lying on the ground. Then the servant raised his weapon, ready to fight back.

Before he could swing at Peter, before an all-out battle could begin, Jesus raised His voice. "Am I leading a rebellion?" He cast a fiery look at the bleeding man and then at Judas and the others. "That you have come out with swords and clubs to capture Me?"

Peter was ready to finish the fight. He raised his sword over his head, his heart pounding. He might not have stayed awake, but he would battle to the death for Jesus now. They could not arrest Him! Peter wouldn't allow it!

Then Jesus did something Peter would never forget. As the crowd inched forward, wielding their clubs and calling for Jesus's death, the Master bent down, picked up the servant's ear, and replaced it on the man's head. One moment Jesus was holding the bloody piece of flesh in His hand, and the next it was attached right where it had been before. The blood was gone and the man's ear looked perfectly normal.

The servant gasped, clearly too astonished to speak. Peter watched as the man felt his ear and looked at his hands. Then he stared at Jesus, joy and terror etched in his face.

"There! See?" Peter shouted at the mob. Surely this would be the end of their violence. Jesus had just reattached a man's ear to his head. They would believe now, they would back away slowly, apologizing for their mistake. They might even fall to their knees and worship Him the way He deserved.

But instead the crowd started shouting at Jesus again, insulting Him, accusing Him of trickery. The guards grabbed Him. "Come now. You're going before the Sanhedrin."

Determination shone in Jesus's eyes. He raised His voice again. "Every day I was with you, teaching in the Temple courts, and you did not arrest Me."

The soldiers jerked at Him, knocking Him to the ground. Fear seized Peter. This was really happening! They were going to arrest Jesus, regardless of His miracles, despite the proof of their own eyes! Which meant . . . all of their lives were in imminent danger.

The other disciples must've been feeling the same thing, because they all cowered together in a group, shrinking away from Jesus, letting Him take the fall by Himself.

Jesus looked back at them, a look so sad it nearly crippled Peter. This time when the Master spoke, His voice held a very deep sorrow. "The Scriptures must be fulfilled."

At that, panic came over Peter and the other disciples. Jesus could free Himself. He could call down all of heaven's angels to handle the angry mob. Instead He was being led away, taken to the Sanhedrin, where . . .

Peter couldn't finish the thought.

If they were going to kill Jesus, if the Master was going to allow that, then—

"Run!" It was Thomas, shouting at the others. "Run for your life!"

They all took off in different directions, running as fast and hard and far away from Jesus as they could. They would be killed otherwise! Arrested and maybe tortured! Peter tore through a thicket, his sides heaving as he ran. His heart was beating so hard he wondered if he might drop dead mid-sprint. But even as he sprinted, as his feet bled from the thorns in the thicket, Peter couldn't shake the consuming feeling. He was disgusted with himself. Wasn't it only hours earlier that Jesus had told them this would happen? They would all fall away. That's what the Master had said. And every one of them had been shocked at the notion.

Until now.

Peter ran one way and then another. Voices seemed to trail him, and he couldn't catch his breath, couldn't see signs of the other disciples. Where had they gone? Had they been captured, too? Finally Peter couldn't take another step. He stopped and bent over, and only then did he notice the tears on his face. He was crying without even knowing it.

He still couldn't catch his breath. The exertion of the run was nothing to the sickening feeling spreading through his body. What was he doing? Running away from Jesus? How could he consider such a thing? He heard the voices again and he turned toward them.

He must've run in a circle, because the sound was the angry mob, still shouting at Jesus as they led Him away. Peter adjusted his garments and dusted himself off. His feet were still bleeding, but he grabbed a handful of dirt and sprinkled it over the tops of them.

*There,* he told himself. That was more presentable. He had to find out if the crowd of captors had arrested the other disciples, too. He had to know how Jesus was doing. This time, he moved more quietly and straight in the direction of the mob.

A few minutes later he could see them. He kept his distance, terrified to be known as one of the disciples. From every direction, people were running closer, trying to get a look at the Teacher being led to the Sanhedrin. The crowd grew so large that Peter actually felt safer.

No one would notice him amidst the others.

*Peter remembered how he* had moved closer that night, his eyes on Jesus. The Master looked straight ahead, not re-acting when the men with clubs shoved Him to the ground or tripped Him. Peter hated himself for not doing something. He could've run through the middle of the crowd and defended Jesus.

At least that.

Peter reached for his sword again, but this time he remembered Jesus's response. He didn't want His disciples waging war against His captors. Okay, but Jesus wouldn't have wanted His closest followers to run. Not sure what to do or how to help, Peter continued to follow the group—far enough away so no one would recognize him as one of the twelve.

Finally they reached the courtyard of the chief priest. The crowd took Jesus through the gates where the priests, elders, and teachers would come together to decide His fate. Peter stayed as close as he could, warming himself at the fire with a group of citizens and guards.

One after another, the guards brought false witnesses through the gates. Whatever they were saying about Jesus, it was all lies. Peter could hear the people being coached as they entered. And as they left, Peter could see them being applauded for their false testimony.

Word made it back outside to the courtyard that Jesus had acknowledged the truth about Himself. He was the Messiah. The Son of the Blessed One. At that, apparently, the chief priest had torn his clothes, outraged at what he perceived to be blasphemy.

From everything Peter gleaned from the guards and the crowd, the real torture of Jesus began then.

Peter felt dizzy, his mind racing. The air felt thick,

too thick for his lungs. He thought about running into the woods and never looking back, or throwing himself at the gates until someone would let him get to Jesus. But all he could do was stand there, warming his hands, paralyzed by what was happening around him.

One of the servant girls of the chief priest came up to the fire. She stopped and peered closely at Peter. "You!" she sneered at him. Her words were loud and sharp. "You also were with that Nazarene, Jesus!"

Many standing around the fire looked at Peter, narrowing their eyes, curious as to whether the girl was right. Peter felt his legs shake. Everyone was looking at him, waiting for his answer. Surely they would pounce on him and arrest him, too.

Before he could stop himself, Peter shook his head. "I don't know what you're talking about." With all eyes on him, Peter walked away. *Don't move too fast,* he told himself. *Keep calm. Otherwise they won't believe you.*

The voice in his head didn't really feel like his own, but he obeyed it anyway. He moved from the fire to the entryway of the inner courts.

A little while later another servant found him. She shouted louder than the girl moments earlier. "This fellow is one of them!"

"I am not!" He spun and spat the words in her face.

"I don't believe you!" The girl was angry, accusing him with every syllable. But no one seemed to believe her, because no one arrested Peter. The girl must've tired of alerting the people to Peter's presence, because eventually she walked away with a group of other servant girls.

Peter leaned against a wall. What had he done? How could he have denied Jesus that way, right out loud? But then . . . was Jesus really the Messiah? He should've freed Himself and shown all of Jerusalem the truth. So why was He allowing this to happen?

The questions assaulted Peter from every side even as one of those standing near him looked his way. "Hey, you!" The man glanced around, yelling to anyone who would listen. He pointed straight at Peter. "Surely you are one of them, for you are a Galilean! I saw you in the garden with Him!"

In the distance, a rooster crowed. Peter heard it. This was exactly what Jesus had warned him about earlier that night. But still, Peter was too terrified to move. Too afraid to tell the truth about Jesus.

A crowd began to gather around Peter, circling him, looking him up and down. A few of them began to agree with the man. "Yes! He is one of them! This man is a friend of Jesus!"

Peter turned one way and then the other, trapped like an animal. He shouted at them with a ferocity he'd never known. "No! I am not one of them!" He watched the people react. Several of them stepped back, afraid of him. Then Peter called down curses on himself and he swore to them. "I don't know this man you're talking about!"

Immediately from nearby came the haunting sound of a rooster. A rooster crowing for the second time. At that same moment, Jesus was dragged past the gate. His face had been beaten, and He struggled to walk. But even as the sound of the rooster rang through the air, Jesus turned and looked straight at Peter.

Straight through him.

The glance lasted only a moment, but it felt like an eternity to Peter. And in that moment, like a sword through his heart, Peter could hear the words of Jesus once more. *Before the rooster crows twice today, you will deny Me three times.* How could he stand here in the midst of those calling for Jesus's death and deny Him?

Peter felt his heart crumbling within him. Jesus was gone now, dragged off to some other place. And Peter had failed his test. There was nothing he could do now, no way to go back and live the moment again. He had denied the Christ, denied the best friend he'd ever had.

He couldn't stay here. No matter what people thought of him or if they agreed together that Peter was guilty, he didn't care. The only thing consuming him was the devastating certainty of Jesus's prediction. Peter had been warned. And still he had denied Jesus three times.

Peter's feet moved without his feeling them, faster and faster across the courtyard to a quiet place shielded from the gates of the chief priest. There Peter fell to the ground and wept.

Every wonderful thing Jesus had ever done came rushing back. The way He had singled Peter out from the others and called him to follow. Jesus's kind way of giving sight to a blind man and legs to the lame. The tears on the

Master's face when He stood among those grieving the death of Lazarus.

Jesus was kind and good; He was the Healer and the Teacher. But He was also God with them. Messiah. Emmanuel. And Peter had denied Him.

Not once, but three times.

Peter pressed his face to the dirt, and the sobs came over him in waves. He would regret this day as long as he lived. Jesus was the greatest friend Peter had ever had.

But even God couldn't forgive this.

*There was—in Peter—the slightest* bit of hope.

In the days since the resurrection, Peter had clung to one tiny detail. Held on to just one miniscule bit of information from the past days. It gave Peter the slightest sense of possibility, the smallest belief that maybe—just maybe—Jesus had forgiven him.

Not the fact that Jesus had risen from the dead or that He stood in their midst in the upper room. Not the way He had comforted the doubting Thomas that afternoon.

No, the single thing that gave Peter the ability to swim toward Jesus and not away from Him this early morning was something an angel had said to Mary Magdalene. Mary—whose faith in the Savior had never wavered—had been told by the angel to go get the disciples . . . and Peter.

*And Peter.*

There it was. In those two little words, God had expressed an undeserved mercy and grace toward Peter that he had held on to every hour of every day since Jesus had risen from the dead. As if the Messiah wanted Peter to know that even after all he'd done wrong, even after denying Jesus three times, the Savior still loved him. Him, the worst of all the disciples. The least faithful of all the friends of Jesus.

He played the words in his head even now. *And Peter.*

Mary Magdalene had been kind enough to find him in the aftermath of Jesus rising from the dead that morning to tell him what had happened. "I think the angel wanted you to know." She had looked intently at Peter. "He forgives you, Peter. He still loves you."

Now they were finished eating and still Peter wished for a private moment with the Master, a chance to affirm his deep regrets and recommit his life to the Savior. He doubted they would have that moment here, with the other disciples gathered around.

Peter looked at the ground. The heat of the fire put him back in the courtyard of the chief priest, the place where he had denied Jesus. If only he had taken the words of the Teacher more seriously. He would've stayed clear of others that night, stood alone at a distance until he could make sense of what had happened.

He was still wondering if he would ever stand near a fire again without feeling the heat of shame and regret for what he had done to the Savior, when he felt a hand on his shoulder. Peter looked up and there was Jesus. The others were gone, back to the boat, collecting the fish from the net, counting them.

For the first time since Jesus had risen from the dead, it was just the two of them. Peter and the Master. "Lord." Peter fell to his knees, his hands stretched out toward Jesus. "I'm sorry. I'm so sorry."

"My son." Jesus reached out His hand and helped Peter to his feet, much the way He'd done that stormy night out on the waves of the Sea of Galilee. He looked deep into Peter's eyes, His tone compassionate. "Come sit with Me."

"Yes, Lord." Peter felt sick to his stomach. He could say nothing in his defense. They sat across from each other, Jesus's eyes intent. "Simon, son of John, do you love Me more than these?"

"Yes, Lord!" Peter was quick with his answer. This was the moment he'd longed for, his chance to assure Jesus that he still loved Him. He still wanted to be part of the mission ahead. Peter struggled to find his voice. "Lord, You know that I love You."

The wind off the Sea of Galilee grew calm. As if God Himself did not want Peter to miss the deeper meaning in the exchange. Jesus waited, searching Peter's face, his eyes. "Feed My lambs."

"Yes, Lord."

Jesus stood and walked a few steps from Peter. He stared at the other disciples, working near the boat. Then

He walked back and looked straight at Peter again. "Simon, son of John, do you love Me?"

Peter felt confused and a little hurt. First, he preferred the name Peter, since that was the name Jesus had given him. The name Simon was intentional, Peter was sure. A reminder of his old life before Jesus, a sign that Jesus no longer completely trusted Peter's allegiance. Which made sense, of course. After what Peter had done, Jesus had every right to doubt him. Peter bowed his head for a moment and then lifted his eyes to Jesus once more. His voice was softer this time. "Yes, Lord. You know that I love You."

For a few moments Jesus looked at the fire. As if the flames and coals reminded Him, too, of that terrible night. He turned to Peter again. "Take care of My sheep."

Difficult as this was, Peter could feel the hope inside him stirring. Jesus was giving him a command here. Not just reinstating him as a disciple. But reinstating him as Peter. The rock. At least it seemed that way.

Once more Jesus paused. He glanced down at the nail marks in His wrists before turning to Peter one final time. A third time. "Simon, son of John, do you love Me?"

The pain of the moment overshadowed the hope of the Master's message. Three times Jesus had asked him. Once for every terrible time Peter had denied the Savior. "Lord, You know all things. You know that I love You."

This time Jesus nodded. "Feed My sheep." Jesus looked confident now. As if only after the third request could He trust Peter's answer. As if it had taken these three 'times for Peter to know the seriousness of what Jesus was asking.

Jesus stared out at the water again. In the quiet of that moment, Peter ran the details of their conversation again in his mind. Jesus had asked Peter to feed His lambs . . . and to take care of His sheep. And again to feed His sheep. All three were slightly different commands, all of them weightier than Peter could fully grasp.

Peter had no doubt about that.

"Thank You, Lord." Peter turned slightly so he could see Jesus better. The wind had picked up again, bringing with it the smell of fish as the other disciples worked near the shore.

Jesus faced him, a deep sorrow in His eyes, as if the Lord were seeing all that had been, all that was . . . and all that would one day be. He drew a slow breath. "Very truly I tell you, when you were younger you dressed yourself and went where you wanted. But when you are old, you will stretch out your hands, and someone else will dress you and lead you where you do not want to go."

Peter felt the ground fall away beneath him, felt the heat from the fire twice as hot as before. He could picture the scene Jesus painted. It was the scene of a crucifixion. The one that might very likely be waiting for Peter if he accepted the Lord's commands.

For a few painful moments, Jesus looked down at His wrists again. When His eyes met Peter's, He simply said, "Follow Me!"

He would. Peter absolutely would. He wanted to stand at the top of the Temple in the middle of Jerusalem and shout his allegiance for all the city to hear. But even so, his heart pounded hard in his chest. A crucifixion?

Just then John walked up from the shore. He waved to Jesus as he approached.

Peter watched Jesus smile and return the wave. Suddenly he couldn't stop from wondering. Was he the only one who would face a terrible death as part of the cost of following Jesus? Peter stood and looked at John as he approached. In a quiet voice he uttered, "Lord . . . what about him?"

The answer didn't come immediately. Then, with just a quick glance in Peter's direction, Jesus turned toward John. He spoke in a tone quieter than before. "If I want him to remain alive until I return, what is that to you?" Jesus faced Peter squarely. "You must follow Me."

It was a deciding moment, a turning point. Peter could turn and run for his life, return to fishing and never talk about Jesus again. He could put the memory of these past few years out of his mind and move on.

But with everything in him, with every breath he took, no matter the cost, Peter wanted only one thing now. The chance to follow Jesus. And so even though he had no idea what tomorrow might look like, even though pain and torture and death might very well await him, he said the only words he could say.

"Yes, Lord. I will follow You."

\* \* \*

*Peter figured the lesson* was patience.

That's what Jesus must've been teaching them in the days after that breakfast on the beach. Because many mornings passed without any instruction about what they were supposed to do next.

Over the next forty days, Jesus appeared to them here and there—but only to interact with them. There were no instructions or parables, no words from the Master about how they should live out the call to follow Jesus. Because of that Peter practiced patience at a level he'd never considered. Now that he had promised Jesus he would feed the Lord's lambs and take care of His sheep, Peter was anxious to start. He wouldn't let Jesus down this time. Not if it cost him his life.

Finally a day came when Jesus pulled the disciples aside. His look was more serious than any time since He had risen from the dead. "Do not leave Jerusalem, but wait for the gift My Father promised, which you have heard Me speak about."

Peter's heart raced and he felt a rush with every word. This was it. Things were about to get serious. Sure, a small number knew about the salvation of Jesus Christ, about His resurrection and how He alone was the way to heaven. But the rest of Jerusalem was still so confused.

He was ready to tell them. Ready to change the world.

Jesus explained about the Holy Spirit . . . and how in a few days the disciples would be baptized in a different way. They would no longer be disciples—followers. Rather, they would be apostles. Teachers of the ways of the Master.

Peter pressed in closer. "Lord, are You at this time going to restore the Kingdom to Israel?"

Several of the other disciples nodded, also wanting to know. "We've been waiting." Thomas folded his arms. "Everyone's looking for the Kingdom to be restored."

When they fell quiet, Jesus allowed a slight smile. "It is not for you to know the times or dates the Father has set by His own authority. But you will receive power when the Holy Spirit comes on you; and you will be My witnesses in Jerusalem and in all Judea and Samaria." He looked straight at Peter. "And to the ends of the earth."

Peter had a hundred questions. Where should they go to find the gift of the Holy Spirit? How would they take it? And how would the power come on them? Would they have a special cloak to signify the power, the way the religious leaders did? Or would people simply know?

But before Peter could ask a single question, Jesus began to rise, right up into the air. Peter and the others fell to their knees, and a few of them cried out, "Jesus! Don't go!"

A strange set of clouds descended over them, covering Jesus and rising with Him. "Where's He going?" Matthew raised his hands, crying out.

Peter was shaking too hard to focus. Was this it? Was Jesus leaving them for good? How were they supposed to spread His word, teach His ways without Him?

Suddenly as they were looking intently into the sky, two men dressed in white appeared from nowhere and stood beside them. One of them did the talking. "Men of Galilee"—he emanated peace—"why do you stand here looking into the sky?"

No one knew what to say. Jesus was their leader, and now—right before their eyes—He was gone.

The man in white continued. "This same Jesus, who has been taken from you into heaven, will come back in the same way you have seen Him go . . ."

And then—without another word—the men in white were gone.

*Peter took charge, and* no one questioned the fact. They had all heard Jesus tell Peter that the church would be built on him. He would take the lead. But even now he wasn't exactly sure what to do next. They didn't have Judas any longer. Sadly, their former friend had taken his life in the aftermath of guilt over betraying the Savior.

In the absence of Judas, Peter led the others in choosing a twelfth apostle. Matthias.

As the days passed, gratitude filled Peter's heart often. He was grateful for the fact that Jesus had forgiven him and reinstated him, grateful that he would still be in charge of the formation of the church—as if he had never betrayed the Master at all. And of course grateful that eventually the Holy Spirit would come upon them, and when it did, they would have power.

But the waiting was almost more than Peter could take.

When the moment finally happened, they were gathered in the upper room, the same place where they'd hidden after Jesus was crucified. One minute they were sitting around the room, talking, and the next a sudden sound like the blowing of a violent wind came from the air above them. As if it was coming from heaven itself.

The house shook and at first terror filled the faces of all the apostles. Peter braced himself against the wall and then, with a flash of light, something that looked like tongues of fire filled the room and separated. The flames moved with intention through the place and came to rest on each of them.

A feeling of peace and love and joy and power filled Peter to overflowing. Then without understanding exactly what was happening, he began to speak in a language not his own. All around him, the other apostles were clearly experiencing the same thing. Each of them was practically shouting in different languages.

Suddenly they felt led to leave the upper room and head into the city streets. In a wild rush and probably drawn by the shouts coming from so many different languages, thousands of people, even the God-fearing Jews from every nation, circled around Peter and the others, hushing each other so they could hear.

And as they heard, they were shocked, amazed because a group of common Galileans were speaking in each of their native tongues. But then a crowd gathered along one side of the circle, laughing and making fun of Peter and the others. "They've had too much wine! Look at those crazy followers of Jesus!"

Others joined in. "You can't believe a word they say. They're drunk!"

"Yeah!" Still others joined in the mockery. "They think Jesus rose from the dead!"

Peter had heard enough.

Amidst the utter chaos breaking out around him, and with thousands of people looking at the friends of Jesus, Peter scrambled up onto a nearby platform and held up both hands. The other eleven took their place with Peter on the platform. It took time, but gradually the crowd stilled until they were practically silent.

Peter raised his voice. "Fellow Jews and all of you who live in Jerusalem, let me explain this to you." He anchored his feet on the rock beneath him. In a beautiful rush, Jesus's words consumed his heart. *You are Peter, and on this rock I will build My church* . . . Peter stood tall and found his focus. "Listen carefully to what I say! These people are not drunk, as you suppose. It's only nine in the morning! No . . . this is what was spoken by the prophet . . ."

As if he had been born for this moment, words began to flow from Peter, words that explained the message of the prophets of old, that everyone who calls on the name of the Lord will be saved. Peter raised his voice a little more. "Fellow Israelites, listen to this: Jesus of Nazareth was a man accredited by God to you by miracles, wonders and signs, which God did among you through Him." He paused for a long moment. "As you yourselves know."

A thought flickered through Peter's mind as he spoke. He hoped the servant girl was in the crowd, the one who had accused him of being a follower of Jesus the night the Master was arrested. Peter might have denied Jesus that awful hour around the fire, but not anymore.

Not ever again.

Passion filled his tone as he talked about the Scriptures and prophecies that proved Christ was the Savior. Not once did Peter's voice waver. The entire time he could picture Jesus's face before him. He could see the sincerity in His grace-filled eyes as He asked Peter to feed His lambs.

Feed them not with food, but with truth.

He was wrapping up his message. He'd explained about Jesus being from the line of David and how His life and death lined up completely with the prophecies. But the most important part was just ahead. Peter looked intently at the faces gathered around the platform. Some of them were getting it. He could see that. Peter drew a long breath and his voice rang with passion. "Therefore, let all Israel be assured of this . . ." Again he paused, letting every word hit its mark in the hearts of the people. "God has made this Jesus, whom you crucified, both Lord and Messiah."

A cry rose up from the people, the first collective response they'd made since Peter started talking. The sound grew and Peter could feel their pain, sense their grief and remorse. They had killed the Savior. They had turned their back on the greatest friend they'd ever had in their midst.

Peter understood their pain. No one could relate to the alarmed crowd more than he could. He had felt this same pain, felt it to his core, around the heat of a fire outside the gates of the Sanhedrin.

The people began calling out to Peter and the other apostles. "Brothers, what shall we do? How do we go on?"

Despite the deep emotion welling in Peter, he found his voice. "Repent and be baptized, every one of you, in the name of Jesus Christ. For the forgiveness of your sins."

Hope shone in the eyes of some of the people. Peter swallowed his own emotion. There was more. "Do this and you will receive the gift of the Holy Spirit."

He held out both hands and looked toward the sky. "The promise is for you and your children and for all who are far off—for all whom the Lord our God will call!"

And suddenly Peter knew.

This was it, the reason Jesus had allowed him to continue as one of the apostles. Right here—in this very moment—the church was beginning. The message of the Savior was taking root. Peter could feel it. The people were still watching him, still waiting. For the next thirty minutes he warned them and pleaded with them. "Save yourselves from this corrupt generation."

All at once the message seemed to sink in—at least for some of the people. The ones who accepted Peter's message. At first twenty and then a hundred, then about three thousand headed for the water. There they were baptized—the ones who had chosen repentance and salvation through Jesus.

When the day ended, Peter found a quiet place outside the city, knelt near a cluster of trees, and wept. Not the weeping that he'd done when he'd been guilty of betraying Jesus, back when he'd had no hope. But a weeping because he loved the people, and because three thousand of them had been saved this very day. Saved from eternal death and destruction. All because of Jesus.

Yes, Jesus had shown him how to lay down his life for other people, how to be a friend the way the Master had been a friend. Even for the people who had mocked Jesus. Peter lifted his eyes to the starry night and felt the power and peace of the Holy Spirit within him. His life would be lived for Jesus now. Ever and always. And one far-off hour—when Peter might be led someplace he didn't want to go, when he might die in a way he didn't want to die— Peter would be okay with that, too.

Because Jesus had taught him the truth about real friendship. He had taught it and demonstrated it when He died on the cross. And Jesus had shown His friendship in one more powerful, unforgettable way.

Jesus had forgiven him.

## CHAPTER 6

# John, the Arrogant Disciple

... And Jesus, the Friend Who
Transforms Through Love

*They were headed to Samaria,* John and Peter. To the very place and people John had once despised. They were headed there to lay hands on the Samaritans and tell them the good news about Jesus, the hope for salvation and the certainty of heaven.

John figured this journey was all the proof anyone could ever need that Jesus had transformed him. But there were so many more signs as well. The change in John wasn't merely the gentler way he had with people. It was something deeper.

The Master had taught John how to love. Not just in actions, but from the heart. He had always done good deeds for others—mostly to be noticed. He'd been good at making his outward appearance shine bright. But now John actually cared about people. He cared about their pain and suffering, and he cared that they know the saving message of hope in Jesus Christ. John had learned what real love looked like, what it felt like.

There could be no other explanation for this trip to Samaria.

John and Peter pushed forward. Since Jesus had returned to heaven, they spent most of their time on the road. Literally. Moving from one city to another, preaching the Good News of the Savior to all the regions of Israel. This particular journey would be seventy-five miles each way, from Jerusalem through the hill country of Judea and north into Samaria. They were headed up a hill now as John turned and studied his friend.

Whatever the changes in John, Peter's were even more dramatic. Back when they all fished together for a living, Peter had been the loudest mouth in the group. Quick to anger, slow to listen. He had been the boldest for Jesus, yes. But Peter had also been the most likely to blurt out the wrong thing. The way he'd done several times—but worst of all in the hours after the arrest of Jesus.

If Peter and John could be halfway to Samaria, headed there to pray for the very people they had spent their lives despising, then this much was true: With Jesus anything was possible.

John kicked at a loose rock as they walked. "You ever think about how it all began? How Jesus chose us out of everyone fishing on the Sea of Galilee that day?"

"Mmmm, yes." Peter glanced at him. "Jesus is God. So I guess He knew who would be the most willing . . . and who needed the most work."

"True." John released a lighthearted laugh. Then he peered at the desert landscape ahead. "My ideas were so selfish back then. Sometimes I wonder who I'd be if Jesus hadn't found me."

"I'd be dead." Peter wasn't laughing now. "Too stubborn to come off the rough seas. Or one too many fistfights down at the seashore."

John nodded. "You're probably right." He sighed. "I don't know, I might've become a teacher. But for all the wrong reasons." John kept walking. He stared at his sandals for a long while, and then up at Peter. "I thought I had all the answers. I wanted everyone to know it."

"Yes." Peter took a swig of water from his bag. "We were very opinionated."

The conversation fell off. Sometimes while they walked they talked at length. Other times they grew silent, and when they did, John loved nothing more than looking back. Nothing better than remembering how it began. Because the John he'd been back then was so entirely different from the John he was today.

John stared at the clear blue sky and the years fell away once more. He and his older brother, James, worked with Peter on the Sea of Galilee. Peter was the wild card back then. He was strong and fierce on the water, the best fisherman in the region.

But John and his brother were smarter. Their parents—

Zebedee and Salome—were people of wealth and means. The two of them were the financial support behind the two boats—the one Peter captained, and the one John and James shared. James had been satisfied with a career of fishing. Most of the time his aspirations didn't go much beyond making a good catch.

John had been different.

He had figured he'd fish for a few years, save up his money. And then maybe find his way into leadership. Local politics or religious duties. Something that would set him apart. He figured one of the first things he'd do was make a new law against the Samaritans.

At that time there had been a group of Samaritans who were encroaching on the fishing market. They would set up camp on the north side of the Sea of Galilee, but lately they'd moved their boats south toward Jerusalem. John had wanted them gone. He despised the Samaritans.

Even though John was working his parents' fishing boat when Jesus entered his life, it certainly wasn't where he expected to wind up. He had big plans.

From the time they were little, his mother had told both him and James that they were destined for greatness. John had always believed her. Especially as he grew older. Peter might've been the strongest fisherman in the area, but John was the most handsome and well-spoken. He was also one of the youngest. Cocky and confident. Better than others. He thought that way about himself constantly.

But he had also known there was something happening in the region. Something spiritual. He and James and Peter had gone to see John the Baptist on several occasions. John had spoken of a Messiah to come, one who would exceed any ordinary person.

John liked to think he was in the know, one of those on the inside of life. More intelligent, more aware. A quick thinker—open to the newest ideas of the day. Certainly after hundreds of years of silence from the prophets, it was a crazy notion to think the Savior might come in their lifetime, let alone soon. But the idea was interesting.

Jesus had found them on the Sea of Galilee. He had been preaching to the people on the seashore, and the crowd grew so large, the Teacher needed to create space for Himself. Which He had done by climbing into Peter's boat.

The invitation to follow came shortly after.

Back then as Jesus gathered His disciples, everyone responded to His invitation differently. Yes, they had all laid down trades and careers and immediately followed Him. But the impact Jesus had on them was different for each.

For John, he had been absolutely convinced from the beginning that Jesus was the Messiah, the Chosen One. He had never been more sure of anything. Peter and James felt the same way. But it had taken John most of the next three years to understand what it meant to be a disciple.

To truly follow Jesus.

*   *   *

*The first time John* recognized how different he was from
the man Jesus wanted him to be was about a year after he
started following Jesus. The Master had sent the disciples
out to neighboring towns with His authority to drive out
demons and to cure diseases, to proclaim the Kingdom of
God and to heal the sick.

John remembered the high he felt when they actually
were able to do what Jesus had commissioned them to do.
He felt almost like Jesus when he and James and Peter
went from one village to the next performing miracles in
Jesus's name. They were famous, really. People came to
them, calling out to them and crowding them wherever
they went.

The feeling of power and greatness was what John
had always expected he'd have one day. He had expected
it to happen in the fishing town where he lived. But healing people, driving out demons, this was far better. This
was the life! They were adored by the people. John didn't
want to brag, but whenever the disciples would meet up,
he had the sense that he had healed more people, driven
out more demons. Almost like he had been given a slightly
stronger sense of power than the other disciples.

Regret filled John's heart as he thought back on that
time. He had been so full of himself. It had been a heady
feeling, knowing everyone was talking about him and the
others. But maybe him a little more. He was the head
turner, the youngest. He had figured if he kept beating out

the other disciples for most healings, if he kept performing better than the others, one day soon Jesus would make him the leader.

Some sort of official title—Best Disciple. Or First Follower.

John had been ready for the applause.

When they all came back together and headed to Bethsaida, Jesus multiplied food for the crowd. He fed five thousand men with a handful of fish and a few loaves of bread. Word about their group was spreading and John couldn't have been happier.

Forget politics. He was a disciple of Jesus!

That day they shared a deeper moment after the meal was over. Jesus brought the disciples to a private place and looked at them with serious eyes. "Who do the crowds say I am?"

John looked from Peter to James and then the others. He shrugged. "Some say John the Baptist; others say Elijah." He looked around again and then back at Jesus. "Still others say You're one of the prophets of long ago come back to life."

Jesus didn't blink. "But what about you? Who do you say I am?"

It took John a minute to clear his head and think about the question. Nearly every waking hour he was obsessed with one thought: how great he had become. John the disciple. John the most talented of Jesus's followers. But who was Jesus? He was the Chosen One, of course.

But before John could put his ideas into words, Peter

stood and made the declaration. "God's Messiah. You're God's Messiah."

Never had John felt jealous of Peter—until that moment. But John didn't have time to think about it or correct himself or find something witty to say that might return the attention and light to himself. Jesus was talking to them again, this time about the suffering He was yet to face.

Jesus made sure He had their attention. "Whoever wants to be My disciple must deny themselves and take up their cross daily and follow Me." Then He looked straight at John. "For whoever wants to save their life will lose it, but whoever loses their life for Me will save it."

Lose their life for Him.

The memory of those words had stayed with John ever since. But the impact of them didn't hit him until much later. John still wanted to be the best, to live out the dream he had imagined for himself when he was younger. And it was with that same mind-set that eight days later John joined James and Peter as part of an inner circle that traveled up onto a mountain to pray. *I've made it now,* John thought. *Surely I can impress the Master more than James and Peter.*

But even as John had been thinking those things, the appearance of Jesus changed, and His clothes became as bright as lightning. Suddenly two men appeared in glorious splendor, talking with Jesus.

Moses and Elijah.

John fell to the ground at the same time as Peter and

James—all of them clearly gripped by shock, disbelieving their eyes. John's mind spun and the words and colors around him blurred together. Gradually he felt himself regaining full consciousness, about the same time Peter and James came to.

They sat up together, and there was Jesus—in all His glory, talking to Moses and Elijah. John had wondered if he was dreaming. If they were all dreaming. Or maybe it was some sort of vision. Peter managed to get to his feet. "Lord"—he nodded, his enthusiasm bubbling over—"it is good for us to be here!"

John had seen this sort of thing before with Peter. Part of the reason they had loved working with the man back in their days as fishermen was his boldness. His way of presenting ideas before he actually sorted through them. But now John cringed as Peter blurted out his thoughts.

"I have an idea!" Peter's words tumbled out one on top of the other, his voice loud. "If You wish, I will put up three shelters." He used his hands to illustrate the sort of structure he was picturing. "One for You, one for Moses, and one for Elijah."

John put his hands over his face. He wanted to shout at Peter and tell him to get back onto his knees. This wasn't some festival, with Jesus, Moses, and Elijah on display in various booths. He shook his head, dreading whatever might come next.

Even while Peter was still speaking, still interrupting the Master's conversation with Moses and Elijah, a bright cloud came over them. John could no longer see his hand in front of his face—the light was that bright. Then a booming voice filled the air and shook the ground. "This is My Son, whom I love; with Him I am well pleased! Listen to Him!"

God Himself had spoken! John trembled on the ground, but as the cloud lifted the message was unmistakable:

Listen.

Peter must've picked up on the fact, too, because he hit the ground facedown right next to John and James. No question all of them were terrified. And even Peter didn't dare speak. They remained on the ground, faces in the dust, until John felt a touch on his shoulder. He opened his eyes just enough to see Jesus standing beside him. Jesus the way He usually looked. Moses and Elijah were gone and so was the bright cloud. Jesus's smile was kind and understanding. "Get up," He said. "Don't be afraid."

He touched the shoulders of Peter and James also, and all three of them struggled to their feet. John felt drained. Adrenaline still raced through his body, making his arms and legs weak and unstable. Peter cast a glance at each of them, his eyes wide. What had just happened? And was that God the Father actually speaking to them a moment ago?

They knew the answer was yes, it had all just happened. The memory would certainly stay with them until their dying days. The walk back down the mountain was quiet for the first several minutes. Just the wind through the canyons and the occasional birds overhead. The seriousness of what they'd witnessed, the reality of Jesus as the Messiah had clearly left them all speechless.

Jesus spoke first. He looked at the three of them and drew a slow breath. "Don't tell anyone what you have seen." His voice was compassionate, but firm. "Not until the Son of Man has been raised from the dead."

Raised from the dead? John hated when Jesus talked this way. Because a person couldn't be raised from the dead unless he first died. And in the case of Jesus, He was clearly referring to His own death. The thought was terrifying. He had told them the religious leaders would put Him to death. What would become of a people who killed their very own Messiah?

What terrible times were ahead? The question made John sick to his stomach—whether he was the best disciple or not.

*The memory faded. John* wiped the sweat off his brow. "Hotter than usual." He turned to Peter. "How much longer?"

"Two days—give or take." Peter took a drink of his water. "I was thinking about Jesus."

"Me, too." John turned his eyes straight ahead. "The transfiguration."

"Hmm." Peter nodded, still setting the pace. "I was remembering that breakfast on the beach. After He rose."

They walked in silence for a few minutes. "Jesus defined love."

"Yes." Peter smiled. "He taught me everything I know

about loving people." A quiet chuckle came from him. "How could we be on the road to Samaria if we didn't have the love of Christ living inside us?"

"So true." John narrowed his eyes and peered ahead at the horizon. He had hated the Samaritans so deeply. Detested how they had encroached on the local fishing business and how they had intermarried with non-Jews. They were the lowest of the low class.

Only Jesus could've changed John's mind about that. The truth took him back to that day again, coming down the mountainside with Jesus, Peter, and James after seeing the transfiguration of the Lord.

That day they had reached the bottom of the mountain and found a large crowd and some sort of disturbance. John had wished for time alone with Jesus and the other disciples, a chance to share what they'd seen. Instead the people rushed at Jesus.

One man yelled out, "Teacher, I beg You to look at my son, for he is my only child." The man pointed to a young boy, maybe ten years old, thrashing about in the dirt. His body continually convulsed and he was foaming at the mouth. Tears streamed down the man's face. He was clearly tormented by the awful sight of his son. The man continued, his words heavy with sorrow. "See? A spirit seizes him and he suddenly screams. It throws him into convulsions so that he foams at the mouth." The man shook his head, nearly frantic. "It scarcely ever leaves him."

The child thrashed worse than before, scratching at himself and looking more like an animal than a human being. John had seen the demon-possessed before but this was one of the worst cases any of them had come across. John's heart ached. He hadn't wanted the distraction of the people, but the sight was almost more than any of them could bear to watch.

Jesus took a step closer to the boy and the crowd stepped back just enough to clear a circle around them. Seeing Jesus move toward them made the boy's father even more adamant. "Teacher, I tell You . . . the spirit hardly ever leaves him." He pointed at his son again. "It is destroying him." He took a few rough swipes at his tears and then nodded toward the other disciples, the ones who hadn't gone up on the mountain with Jesus. Desperation filled the man's tone. "I begged your disciples to drive it out, but they could not."

A heaviness came over Jesus as He looked from the disciples to the boy, still convulsing on the ground. Jesus's expression darkened in a way that showed the sadness in His soul. When He spoke, His voice was tinged with defeat. "You unbelieving and perverse generation." He searched the faces gathered around Him. "How long shall I stay with you and put up with you?"

The words were harsh, but Jesus didn't seem harsh as He said them. John felt a little guilty. If he had been here and not up on the mountain with Jesus, then surely he would've had no trouble casting out the demons. But so many people didn't really believe the way John believed. Of course Jesus was frustrated. John shook his head. The other disciples had so much to learn.

So Jesus sighed and took a step closer to the father and his boy. "Bring your son here."

The man helped his child to his feet, but even while the boy was trying to make his way toward Jesus, the demon threw him to the ground in convulsions.

Jesus raised His hand toward the boy. "Out! Be gone from him!"

Instantly the boy fell in a heap on the ground, completely still. A gasp came from the crowd. No matter how many times they witnessed the miracles of Jesus, nothing could prepare them for this, watching Jesus cast out a demon by the power and authority of His words. The crowd held its breath, because it looked like the boy was dead. John took a step closer, studying the child. He was so very still.

But Jesus lowered Himself to the boy and took his hand. "Get up, My son. You are healed."

With that the boy opened his eyes and easily stood. He dusted off the dirt from his clothes as if nothing had happened. As if he hadn't been thrashing about on the ground just moments earlier. But the boy knew. Because he hugged Jesus around the neck and looked straight into His kind eyes. "Thank You, Jesus."

The Master smiled in return. "Follow Me."

"Yes." The boy nodded. "Always."

Jesus led the boy by the hand and gave him to his father. "Here is your son."

The man's mouth hung open and he was stone still. As if the shock was too great to move or speak or even acknowledge the amazing thing that had just happened. The boy wrapped his arms around his father's waist. "I love you, Daddy."

At the sound of his son's voice, the man pulled his boy close to himself. He held him in a desperate embrace. His boy had been all but dead. Now he was whole and healthy. Alive. The father turned to Jesus. "Thank You." He fell to his knees and lifted his hands to heaven. "Glory to You, God. You are great and Your Messiah is the Holy One!"

Chills ran down John's arms. Again he was grateful to be here, to witness the Teacher return a child to his father. All eyes were on Jesus and the disciples. John couldn't help but think the obvious: He wasn't only a disciple. He was one of the inner three, the closest friends of Jesus. People had seen the three of them come down the mountainside with Jesus, right? So everyone in the crowd knew that John wasn't an ordinary disciple. He wasn't one of the ones who had failed this child.

He was special.

More than that, he had the financial means to lead them as the movement of Jesus grew. And since he had shown the common sense to stay quiet in the midst of the transfiguration, it must've seemed apparent to Jesus that he was the best disciple. Definitely. Top of his game.

These thoughts came in a hurry, even as the crowd was falling to its knees and praising God. But while everyone was worshiping Jesus and thanking God for the miracle they'd just witnessed, Jesus pulled the disciples aside. "Listen carefully to what I'm about to tell you: The Son of Man is going to be delivered into the hands of men."

Tears welled up in Peter's eyes. John wasn't sure what exactly Jesus meant, but if hardship was coming, if Jesus was about to be taken from them, maybe this was the moment to establish his place as the lead disciple. He stepped into the middle of their gathering. "I believe this is a good time to suggest something." John didn't hesitate. "When Jesus goes, I'll be the leader. The Master views me as the greatest of the disciples, so if we can just agree on that now, it'd be—"

"What?" His brother James pressed his way closer, his nose inches from John's. "You're not the greatest! I'm older than you." He looked around at the other disciples and then back to John. "Clearly, *I'm* the greatest."

John raised his voice. "The greatest of the disciples has to be one of us three." He motioned to Peter and James. "Jesus includes us more than the rest of you. And among us three, I'm obviously the strongest choice because—"

"Friends." That single word from Jesus stilled the debate. The little boy who had been healed moments earlier came running up to thank Jesus again. Jesus looked at the disciples as He put His arm around the child. "Whoever welcomes this little child in My name, welcomes Me. And whoever welcomes Me, welcomes the One who sent Me." He looked at John, straight through him, really. "For whoever is the least among you will be the greatest."

Confusion clouded John's heart and mind. He had barely noticed the child running up to Jesus. And now what was Jesus trying to say? The least would be greatest? That didn't make sense. The least of them all couldn't fund them, or lead an army and command a charge in Jesus's defense.

John blinked, embarrassed. He tried to think of something to change the topic, to divert attention from the indirect reprimand he'd just received. Then something hit him. "Master." He crossed his arms. "We saw someone driving out demons in Your name and we tried to stop him. Because he is not one of *us*."

There. That would do the trick. Maybe Jesus simply needed to remember the importance of the team. A team Jesus Himself had gathered. Of course they were great. They were the ones with power to drive out demons and heal the sick. That power didn't belong to someone as ordinary as a little boy.

But even as John was reassuring himself with those thoughts, Jesus turned to him. "John, do not stop them. For whoever is not against you is for you."

What? John wanted to argue, wanted to remind Jesus of the special abilities He had given the twelve disciples. Only them. But he kept quiet. Over the next few days John felt out of sorts. He was the greatest . . . he had no doubt.

But somehow Jesus had missed that fact.

\*    \*    \*

*John hated remembering the* arrogance of his ways back then. But remembering was one way John could celebrate his gratitude for how completely Jesus had changed him.

How patient Jesus had been with him. How grateful John remained every waking hour for the forgiveness and grace and transforming power of the Messiah. For even after Jesus explained that John must be the least if he were to be the greatest, John still didn't give up. Instead he had come up with a plan. John could see himself again, his determination and persistence in asserting his own greatness.

Back then as the days passed, John had pulled his brother James aside. "Okay." He looked around, making sure none of the other disciples could hear him. "You and I both believe we're the greatest."

"I'm the oldest." James scowled at him. He'd kept his distance from John all week.

"I know, I get it." John kept his voice low. "But Jesus has room on either side of Him, right? So what about this . . ."

After he'd detailed the plan to James, and after James had reluctantly agreed to share the position of greatest with John, the two of them went to Jesus. John took the lead, since this was his idea. "Teacher, we want You to do for us whatever we ask."

A long pause followed. When Jesus finally spoke, there was the slightest disbelief in His voice. "What do you want Me to do for you?"

"Well"—John looked at James and then back at

Jesus—"let one of us sit at Your right hand and the other at Your left in Your glory."

"Yes!" James nodded his agreement.

Jesus only stared at John and James before He finally shook His head. "You don't know what you are asking." Jesus rubbed His hands together, looking at His wrists. He looked more intent when He lifted His eyes to John again. "Can you drink the cup I drink, or be baptized with the baptism I am baptized with?"

John didn't give a single moment's thought to the question. "We can." He nodded confidently. "Absolutely."

For a long minute Jesus looked to the sky. Then He exhaled slowly and explained that yes, one day they would drink from His cup and be baptized in the way that Jesus would. But the places at His left and right were not for Him to grant.

John had expected some resistance from Jesus. His mother was part of the group of followers of Jesus, so he motioned for her to join them. While James was talking to the Master, John spoke quietly to his mother. He explained the situation. "Could you ask Him? He won't listen to us."

"Of course." John's mother moved toward Jesus, waiting for a break in the conversation between Him and James.

John smiled to himself. His mother would do the trick. She had always thought her boys would be great. She had the money to make sure her boys were successful. Politicians or community leaders. Religious officials.

Something important. And John, most of all. He lifted his chin, confident as he waited.

At the first possible moment, John watched his mother fall to her knees at the feet of Jesus. "Lord . . ." She bowed her head.

The Master turned to her. "What is it you want?"

She held both hands up to Him, adoring Him. "Grant that one of these two sons of mine may sit at Your right and the other at Your left in Your Kingdom." She paused. "Whatever it costs, I can see that You are paid."

About that time, Matthew and Thomas cried out, "What's this?"

The other disciples joined in, curious. "What are you asking the Master?"

Matthew scowled. "They're asking for the top places, the spots of honor at the Lord's right and left side!" he snapped the words in the direction of John and James. "Are you serious?" He waved his hand at John's mother. "And having your *mother* make the request for you? This is unacceptable."

"You're not the greatest, John. You either, James," Thomas shouted. The other disciples joined in.

Another argument broke out, and John wondered if this time he had pushed things too far. Yes, he wanted to be the greatest. But if the other ten disciples were against him and James, then this plan could never work.

Again Jesus began teaching them. He spoke about the

officials and religious leaders lording their power over those beneath them. "Not so with you." Peace filled His words as He looked deeply into the eyes of each of them and finally at John. "Instead, whoever wants to become great among you must be your servant. And whoever wants to be the first must be slave of all."

Jesus stood and came face to face with John. "For even the Son of Man did not come to be served, but to serve. And to give His life as a ransom for many."

The words of Jesus silenced the men. John had failed again. The disappointment felt bitter to the depths of his soul. Jesus motioned for them to follow Him, and as they were leaving, the crowd gathered around them again. Two blind men were sitting by the roadside, and when they heard that Jesus was about to pass by, they shouted, "Lord, Son of David, have mercy on us!"

John was tired of the people. They were always pressing in around Jesus, always asking for some kind of help. Jesus and His friends hadn't had a truly quiet moment in forever. The crowd shouted for the blind men to be quiet, and John raised his voice above even the mass of people. "Leave the Master alone! Be quiet!"

"No!" The blind men shouted even louder. "Lord, Son of David, have mercy on us!"

At that, Jesus stopped. He walked up to the men and the crowd fell silent once more. The look on Jesus's face was pained. As if it truly broke the Master's heart to see the two suffering blind men. "My friends," Jesus spoke to them, loud enough for John and the disciples and all the crowd to hear. "What do you want Me to do for you?"

Suddenly John recognized the question. It was the same question Jesus had asked John and James earlier that day. *What do you want Me to do for you?* John held his breath, waiting for whatever was coming next.

One of them held up a trembling hand. "Lord!" Tears slid down his cheeks. "We want our sight!"

Jesus took a step closer. He reached out and gently touched the eyes of the man, and then the one beside him. Immediately the men blinked a few times and then they shouted with joy.

"I can see!" The one turned to the other. "We can see! Jesus, You are the Messiah!"

John felt his footing turn liquid beneath him. His heart crashed to his knees and he pulled himself to the edge of the crowd. What had just happened? Suddenly John began to understand. Jesus had granted a request from two beggars, two dirty old blind men.

Yet, He had denied the request by John and James.

He stumbled to a place near a stone building and pressed his face against the wall and the truth hit him like so many stones. Jesus wasn't interested in which disciple was the greatest. He had treated with more kindness the request of the blind men. John had the strangest feeling that he also was receiving his own sight for the first time. He felt humbled and embarrassed and ashamed of his request to be the greatest.

The blind men only wanted one thing—the chance to see Jesus.

Which was maybe what Jesus had wanted from John all along.

*If only John had* entirely learned his lesson that afternoon.

Over the coming days, John thought often of how the least would be the greatest. He pictured the way the blind men had been granted sight—and how the first beautiful sight they saw was the face of Jesus. But as the time came for the Passover, and as Jesus and the disciples headed for Jerusalem, the Master again showed John that his heart was still not right.

That day Jesus sent messengers ahead of them to a Samaritan village to get things ready. As they traveled south to Jerusalem, news came back to them that the Samaritans there did not welcome Him. One of the messengers explained the reason. "Master, they know You are headed to Jerusalem. And Samaritans do not associate with Jews."

John's anger was quick and intense. How dare the Samaritans refuse to welcome Jesus? James was angry, too. The brothers pushed their way past the other disciples to Jesus. John did the talking, his tone strong and sharp. "Lord, do You want us to call fire down from heaven to destroy them?"

No doubt, John was ready. He gritted his teeth and stared in the direction of Samaria. "It's about time someone took care of those—"

"John." Jesus raised His voice. "That's enough. You will not speak like that again."

The rebuke silenced John, and again sent him humiliated to the back of the group of Jesus's followers. They traveled through a different village, and all the while John thought the Master had perhaps lost His mind. The Samaritans had been a thorn in the side of God's holy people long enough. This would have been the perfect time to rid the region of them—once and for all.

Yet Jesus chose to show them mercy.

It was more than John could comprehend.


*They were almost to* Samaria, the landscape and smells, the sights all a familiar reminder of those final days with Jesus. Back when John had still not completely understood the Master's teachings.

"I was so hard-hearted." John turned to Peter. They were walking faster now, trying to make the crest of the next hill before nightfall.

Peter nodded, a knowing look in his eyes. "We both were."

"Jesus gave those blind men their sight, and still I couldn't see." John lifted his face to the heavens as they continued. "Jesus was so patient."

"True." Peter's voice emanated peace. "Then and now."

The realization hit John hard. It was true. Jesus had loved the Samaritans back then, and clearly He loved them still. Otherwise He wouldn't have empowered John and Peter to go to Samaria and pray for the people there.

A clear moment stood out in John's mind. "I remember when it hit me, everything Jesus tried to tell me about the least being the greatest."

Peter looked at him, waiting.

"It was at the last supper we had together." Emotion made John's throat tighten. He could see that time again, the way Jesus handled His approaching murder with resolve and strength. He coughed a few times, struggling to find the words. "When Jesus washed our feet." A single tear slid down his cheek and he caught it with his rough fingertips.

"Yes." Regret colored Peter's expression. "I wanted Him to stop, remember?"

"I felt the same way." John could see himself, the way he had almost lunged forward, joining Peter with a shout that Jesus stop serving them. "Before I could ask the Lord to back away from me, the truth hit." A sad laugh came from him. "Jesus was the greatest. And if He could serve us by washing our feet, then we had to do the same for other people. We had to be like Him."

They walked in silence again, John caught up in the memory of that time. By nightfall they had reached the hilltop area and made camp. John remembered making eye contact with Jesus as the Master washed his feet. And in that single instant John knew he would never be the same again.

Jesus knew it, too.

Because He asked John to sit next to Him at the dinner that night.

Later, when Jesus was arrested, every other disciple ran for their lives. Even John. But very quickly John rejoined Mary Magdalene and the other women—at peace with being labeled one of Jesus's followers. Regardless of the way people jeered at him and mocked him, he stayed with the women. He protected them from the crowd. And when Jesus was crucified, John was there a few feet away.

Weeping.

He wept because he had missed the point of being a disciple of Jesus for all those seasons, for three straight years. He wept because he wished for more time with the Master. More time to learn and grow and prove to the Lord that he did understand.

But clearly Jesus knew John's heart that day. For in His final minutes, He did something that still shocked John. He handed over His mother, Mary, to John's keeping. John, who had been so arrogant and selfish. Mary now lived in John's home, active among the followers of Jesus. And John looked out for her, the way he would continue to do as long as he lived.

There on the hill, halfway to Samaria, before he fell asleep that night, John pulled out his scroll and began to write. In quiet moments he could feel the Holy Spirit moving within him, prompting him to write an account of all that had happened since the birth of Jesus. An account of Jesus's deity and His Good News.

Peter had been doing the same, writing, to the newly formed churches. One evening a few days ago, Peter had spotted the work John was doing. He read the first page and looked at John. "You didn't write your name."

"No." John didn't explain. He didn't have to. There was nothing wrong with Peter or the other disciples writing their names in the letters and books they were writing. That was fine for them.

But for John, he could not put his name to his writings. They were God's alone. He was nothing. He was the least of these. Jesus was everything. He would write as the Spirit led him as long as he drew breath. Jesus had talked about the hope of His resurrection being for even those far off. Future generations. When those people read John's accounts, they needed to see Jesus. Not John. So he left his name off. That way they would focus on Jesus. How He lived and served. How He illustrated that the least would be the greatest.

Humbly. Serving others. Loving the unlovable. John smiled to himself. Even the Samaritans.

He would tell anyone who might read his work not to love the world or anything in the world. For the things of the world—especially the pride of life—did not come from the Father, but from the world. And whoever might do the will of God would certainly live forever. He would explain that Jesus—the greatest friend of all—had laid down His life for His friends, His followers. And that all of them ought to lay down their lives for each other. Because that's how a true friend loved best.

The way John was doing now—on this trip to Samaria.

Jesus had loved him as a friend when John was filled with pride and arrogance. He had loved him when John deserved nothing but wrath. Jesus had asked him to be the least—not the greatest. To be the kind of friend willing to lay down his own life. John understood that now.

So no matter what God called him to write, no matter how many times the Spirit pressed upon him to tell the story of Jesus, or how often he penned a letter encouraging the churches, John knew this much: He would never sign his name.

Like the blind men, he was no longer walking in darkness.

John could see—and he would spend his life serving people. Loving them. All of them. He was able to love that way now, eyes open, heart willing.

All because of the friendship of Jesus.

# Acknowledgments

A special thanks to my team at Howard Books, Simon & Schuster, and LifeWay for believing in the vision for these Bible stories. I am grateful to be surrounded by such a professional publishing team. This book wouldn't have been possible without all of you.

Thanks also to my unbelievable agent, Alive Communications President Rick Christian. Oh, the dreams we have seen become reality. God's grace and favor and your amazing gifts of persuasion have truly made the difference, Rick. Thank you for believing in me always. And thanks for praying for my family and me.

Of course thank you to my husband and kids for always understanding when I'm on deadline. At the end of this amazing journey, I pray that you all celebrate the fact that the greatest story I ever told was the one I wrote with the days of my life. You are my very favorite characters!

And thanks, most importantly, to God Almighty. The gift is Yours. May I use it to glorify You all the days of my life.

# Questions for Individual Reflection or Group Discussion

If you want to read *The Friends of Jesus* as a Bible study, get the LifeWay *Friends of Jesus* workbook and six-part video teaching!

## CHAPTER I

### Simon, the Leper

. . . And Jesus, the Compassionate Friend

1. What do you think was the worst part of leprosy back in biblical times?

2. How was Jesus a better friend to Simon than his peers at the Temple?

3. What lesson did Simon ultimately learn about friendship from Jesus?

## CHAPTER 2

# Martha, the Broken-Hearted

### ... And Jesus, the Comforting Friend

1. Have you ever stood beside someone you love in a hospital and wondered where God was when you needed Him? Describe that time.

2. Martha was a friend to Jesus, but deep down she didn't fully commit her heart to trusting Him. How does distrust affect a friendship?

3. Jesus showed an unwavering friendship toward Martha and Mary. How do you feel when a friend sits with you and cries with you during hard times?

## CHAPTER 3

# Jairus, the Two-Faced Leader

### . . . And Jesus, the Loyal Friend

1. Jairus had friends who expected perfection out of him. How is a real friend different than this?

2. Jesus never mentioned Jairus's hypocrisy as He led the entourage on the way to heal the man's daughter. How has a friend shown unconditional love to you?

3. When you are in desperate need, where do you turn?

## CHAPTER 4

# Mary Magdalene, the Demon-Possessed

### . . . And Jesus, the Friend Who Restores

1. How do you think Mary Magdalene felt before meeting Jesus?

2. Why wasn't Jesus afraid to approach Mary?

3. Mary showed great friendship to Jesus after her healing. What event in your life helps you relate to Mary?

4. Why do you think Mary was the first person to see the resurrected Jesus?

## CHAPTER 5

# *Peter, the Betrayer*

. . . And Jesus, the Friend Who Forgives

1. What personality traits set Peter apart from the other disciples?

2. What were Peter's strengths? What were his weaknesses?

3. Have you ever had a friend betray you, or have you ever betrayed a friend? Did you learn any lessons in the process?

4. Because of the forgiveness of Jesus, Peter found a healed friendship with Him. How was Peter different after Jesus forgave him?

## CHAPTER 6

# John, the Arrogant Disciple

. . . And Jesus, the Friend Who Transforms Through Love

1. Had you ever thought of John the disciple as being arrogant? What biblical evidence supports this possibility?

2. At some point, John understood what Jesus meant by "The first shall be last, and the last shall be first." What do you think was the turning point for John in his friendship with Jesus?

3. What did you learn about friendship through watching Jesus interact with the characters in this book?

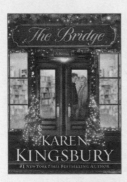

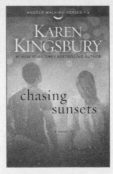

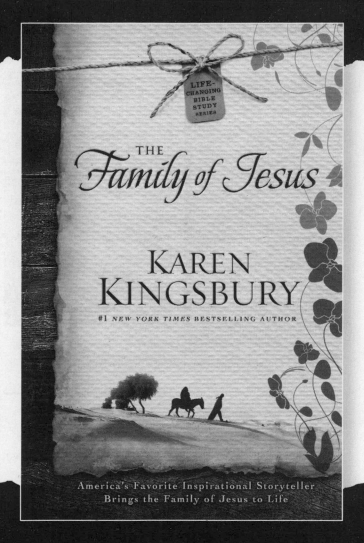

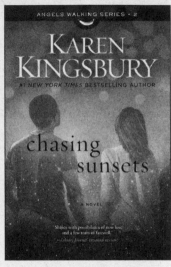